Education and College

William Dudley, *Book Editor*

Teen Decisions

Daniel Leone, *President*

Bonnie Szumski *blisher*

Scott Barbour *ditor*

Hele *itor*

GREENHAVEN
PRESS®

THOMSON
GALE

San Diego • Detroit • New York • San Francisco • Cleveland
New Haven, Conn. • Waterville, Maine • London • Munich

Cover credit: AP Photo/Charles P. Saus

LIBRARY OF CONGRESS CATALOGING-IN-PUBLICATION DATA
Education and college / William Dudley, book editor.
p. cm. — (Teen decisions)
Includes bibliographical references (p.) and index.
ISBN 0-7377-1260-0 (lib. bdg. : alk. paper) —
ISBN 0-7377-1259-7 (pbk. : alk. paper)
1. College choice—United States. 2. Universities and colleges—United States—Admission. 3. Academic achievement—United States. 4. Non-formal education—United States. I. Dudley, William, 1964–
LB2350.5 .E38 2003
378.1'942—dc21   2002026074

Printed in the United States of America

Contents

Foreword

The teen years are a time of transition from childhood to adulthood. By age 13, most teenagers have started the process of physical growth and sexual maturation that enables them to produce children of their own. In the United States and other industrialized nations, teens who have entered or completed puberty are still children in the eyes of the law. They remain the responsibility of their parents or guardians and are not expected to make major decisions themselves. In most of the United States, eighteen is the age of legal adulthood. However, in some states, the age of majority is nineteen, and some legal restrictions on adult activities, such as drinking alcohol, extend until age twenty-one.

This prolonged period between the onset of puberty and the achieving of legal adulthood is not just a matter of hormonal and physical change, but a learning process as well. Teens must learn to cope with influences outside the immediate family. For many teens, friends or peer groups become the basis for many of their opinions and actions. In addition, teens are influenced by TV shows, advertising, and music.

The Teen Decisions series aims at helping teens make responsible choices. Each book provides readers with thought-provoking advice and information from a variety of perspectives. Most of the articles in these anthologies were originally written for, and in many cases by, teens. Some of the essays focus on ethical and moral dilemmas, while others present pertinent legal and scientific information. Many of the articles tell personal stories about decisions teens have made and how their lives were affected.

One special feature of this series is the "Points of Contention," in which specially paired articles present directly opposing views on controversial topics. Additional features in each book include a listing of organizations to contact for more information, as well as a bibliography to aid readers interested in more information. The Teen Decisions series strives to include both trustworthy information and multiple opinions on topics important to teens, while respecting the role teens play in making their own choices.

Introduction

Most teenagers in contemporary American society share the same vocation: that of student. Although many teens have jobs, they are not for the most part expected to work full-time or to support themselves. The idea of dropping out of school at the age of fifteen or sixteen, even to do something generally lauded like entering the workforce or beginning a family, is less socially acceptable than it was in the early 1900s. Teens are instead expected to channel their energies toward their education. U.S. Census data indicates that while only 30 percent of youth age fifteen to seventeen were enrolled in school in 1900, by the 1980s at least 90 percent of this age group were attending school. Education is widely seen as a key to securing a person's future.

The education young people receive during their teen years is in part a result of external circumstances, such as their family situation, socioeconomic standing, and the state of the schools they attend. But it is also a result of choices, large and small, that teens make themselves. As young people progress through their teen years, the array of choices before them regarding their education grows. Although education is a lifelong process, not just something for the young, the decisions one makes in the teen years will have lasting consequences.

Choices Before Sixteen

During the early teen years, the choices and control teens have over their own education is constrained by school policies and state law. Attending school, for example, is not something for only teens and their families to decide. Attendance laws in thirty states make education compulsory for all teens sixteen and under; other states mandate attendance for seventeen- and eighteen-year-olds (or until a person fulfills high school graduation requirements). Choices are also sometimes limited on where teens can receive their education. Those who attend public school (roughly nine out of ten of all high school students) have often in the past had no choice but to attend the school to which they were assigned. In recent years a growing number of school districts have expanded their offerings and have given students the power to choose between any high school in their district, including specialized charter and alternative schools. A minority of American teens get their education from outside the public school system, be it in prep schools, parochial Catholic schools or other religious academies, or home schooling (in many cases, the decision to attend such schools is a choice of the family, not the individual teen).

Once teens have settled on a particular school, they can still affect the course of their education. They generally have greater latitude in choosing what classes to take than they did in elementary and middle school. They can choose how much energy and effort they put into their schoolwork assignments and extracurricular activities.

The Choice to Stay or Drop Out

As teens get older, their education choices expand. One major choice all teens eventually confront is whether to stay in high school. Each year, more than half a million teens drop out of high school without graduating. According to the National Center for Educational Statistics, 12 percent of entering ninth graders fail to graduate from high school. Dropout rates are higher for minority ethnic groups and students from low-income families. In some large urban schools, dropout rates can be as high as 60 percent of the total school population.

Students drop out of school for various reasons. Girls who become pregnant and have children often leave school. Sometimes students drop out to find work to support their families. Others become involved with gangs or drug abuse. Much of the time, however, the reasons are school-related — the students were doing poorly in school and had little hope of doing better. Many dropouts have behavioral disorders and learning disabilities such as attention deficit disorder or dyslexia that may or may not be diagnosed, but which make school more difficult. Many students labeled as "slow" or "troublemakers" feel the way this Oakland teen describes: "I was invisible, man. I knew it. I sat in those schools for two years. I sat in the back of the room and I did nothing. I didn't speak to anyone and no one spoke to me. Nobody said, 'Do your work' or nothing. Then one day I said it, 'Man I'm invisible here.' I got up and walked out the door and I never went back."

Whatever the reason, dropping out of high school can have severe social and economic consequences. This was not necessarily the case in the past, as education professor Michael Harvey writes:

> In the United States' recent past, it was not uncommon for students to complete their schooling after eighth grade and to enter the workforce. There was a labor market advantage to leaving school, going to work, and becoming a wage earner who contributed to one's family and society. For many people, the choice of working was a decision of economic need, personal preference, and employment opportunity.

Harvey goes on to say that the changing social circumstances have increased the negative ramifications of dropping out of high school:

> Times have changed significantly, however. The current work force, driven by a highly technical global society, has different demands and complexities from those of past agrarian and industrial economies. Students who drop out of school today are confronted with significant job competition, work environments driven by significant technical influences, and less than receptive employers. . . . Employment opportunities in today's high skill–high wage economy require advanced skills that dropouts generally do not possess.

In other words, it is very hard for a high school dropout to get a decent job—one that pays enough to live comfortably and has prospects for advancement. Even jobs with skills that appear to have little to do with the high school curriculum, such as auto repair or plumbing, require specialized technical training in institutes that often require a high school diploma as a prerequisite. The U.S. military, once an option for high school dropouts, also generally requires at least a high school education for its recruits.

The importance of a high school education is reflected in labor statistics. The unemployment rate for high school dropouts was 22.5 percent in 1995 versus 12.1 percent for high school graduates, according to the Bureau of Labor Statistics. According to the U.S. Census, the average annual salary earned by high school dropouts in 1996 was $14,013, compared with $21,431 for high school graduates.

The unpromising job market prospects for high school dropouts can hurt other areas of their lives. Many, disillusioned with their job prospects, suffer from low self-esteem and often turn to substance abuse or criminal activity. Almost 80 percent of people in American prisons are high school dropouts, according to a 1995 Department of Corrections survey. "Of course, not every dropout is a criminal or a drug user," says counselor Debra Thorsen. "But being trapped in a life of poor jobs with no hope of growth is not an ego builder."

Alternatives to Dropping Out

What courses of action exist for teens who are struggling in school—or who have already dropped out? One possible option for people without a high school diploma is to earn a GED certification. GED stands for General Education Development tests. Originally developed for returning World War II veterans who wanted to take advantage of federal government support to go to college, but who lacked a high school diploma, these tests have been used to qualify students for college and student-aid programs. By passing the tests, which cover reading, writing, math, science, and social studies, students can receive GED certificates. About three-quarters of a million people take GED tests each year. The average age of a taker is twenty-five; roughly half of those who pass go on to further education or training. Studies have shown that people with a GED earn more on average than high school dropouts—but less than those with a regular high school diploma. "While the GED does open many doors, high school dropouts may be better off with a regular diploma," writes author Elizabeth Weiss Vollstadt. "If they can't succeed in their regular high school, they might look for an alternative school."

A growing number of school districts provide alternative schools. Some are focused on gifted students; others cater to at-risk youth such as teens battling alcoholism. Vollstadt describes several alternative schools in her book *Teen Dropouts*. In the Storefront School in Daytona Beach, Florida, students work individually at their own pace using computers and software learning packages. The Street Academy in Oakland, California, operated by the Bay Area Urban League, creates mentor relationships between teachers and students to help teens who have had trouble in regular high schools. Horizon Education Centers in Orange County, California, creates homelike education sites in a variety of locations, including churches, homes for neglected children, and juvenile detention facilities; it also features small classes and counseling to help at-risk children. Some community colleges have high school diploma programs for older teens. The federal Job Corps program provides residential vocational training. Students who may be interested in such programs should ask their high school counselor about what may be available in their area.

After High School

For those who choose to stay the course and graduate from high school, the big question becomes what happens next. Unlike the situation for younger teens, there are no state laws forcing anyone to go anywhere. But many teens graduate from high school with the expectation that they will continue their education in college. According to a survey by Ferris State University, more than two-thirds of American young people intend to go to a four-year college after graduating from high school. A quarter plan to attend a two-year community college or technical training school. Only 6 percent plan no further schooling.

The college decision is one of the first major decisions many teens make. It is actually more than one single decision on whether or not to go to college. It is a process consisting of numerous decisions, large and small, including what college(s) to apply for, what kind of degree to pursue, what field of study to major in, and how to pay for it all.

The arguments for going to college are similar to those for completing high school. The basic assumption is that education is a necessity for a successful career and a successful life. Some studies have concluded that 80 percent of new jobs being created in America require some sort of training or education beyond high school. A degree from a college or university is a prerequisite for several popular professions, such as medicine, law, engineering, and education. People with some college education have lower unemployment rates and higher average salaries than those with only a high school education. According to the College Board, the company responsible for the SAT, a person with a four-year college degree earns 81 percent more than the average high school graduate—a difference that could add up to more than 1 million dollars over a lifetime.

For many, such monetary concerns are an important but not primary consideration in weighing whether to go to college. A postsecondary education is important for other benefits as well. For some teens, college provides an opportunity to live away from one's family. For others it provides time to settle on career and life plans. Former university president John E. Corbally Jr. writes that education has significant benefits for both teens and society:

> A university or college education helps men and women enjoy richer, more meaningful lives. . . . It . . . gives a person a better appreciation of such fields as art, literature, history, human relations, and science. In doing so, a university or college education enables individuals to participate with greater understanding in community affairs.

However, while many people agree that further education is desirable, there are many options for attaining it (another example of how the array of choices in one's education increase as one gets older). High school students are generally limited to choosing between schools in their community. But after high school they can choose from among thousands of institutions throughout the country and beyond. In 2001 there existed in the United States 4,182 accredited institutions offering academic degrees, including 2,450 four-year colleges and universities and 1,732 two-year colleges. (For many high school juniors and seniors, it may seem as if every one of these institutions is sending them something in the mail.) Part of the decision process many teens endure is narrowing down these thousands of institutions into one or more that they wish to attend.

In addition to deciding *where* to pursue post-secondary education, teens have options on *when*. The standard model has been to enter college the fall after high school graduation. But some teens have been able to deviate from this standard, either by taking college classes (and earning college credit) while still in high school, or by taking one or more years off between high school and college. Alternatives for teens seeking such a "sabbatical" from school include entering the workforce as an intern or employee, starting one's own business, volunteer work, foreign travel, or military service. Many colleges will accept students and allow them to postpone attending school to pursue such activities. The opportunity to educate oneself through college will exist long after one's teen years are over. Much as high school dropouts can later work to obtain a GED, teens who do not go to college (or who drop out after a year or two) often are able to complete their college education later.

A Three-Step Process

For high school students who have decided to go to college, but don't know where, college advice counselor Joyce Slayton Mitchell recommends a three-step decision process. The first is self-assessment. Students should have a clear idea of what they want out of college and how strong their academic credentials (including grades and SAT scores) are. The next step is researching colleges and attempting to match which college best fits one's needs. Mitchell's third step, communicating with colleges, involves the application process in which high school students introduce themselves to the colleges they have chosen.

Students considering college should have a clear idea not only of the strength of their academic record, but also their goals and values—what they want out of college and how hard they are willing to work for them. Teens should identify their interests (both in and out of the classroom). They should assess how independent and self-disciplined they are (self-starters may thrive in larger colleges, while those who need more guidance may do better in smaller schools). They need to ask themselves whether they wish to remain at home or move away, and how far they wish to move from home. If a student knows exactly what subject she wants to major in or what career path to follow, she should investigate colleges with good reputations in that particular field. If, like many teens, she is unsure of what she wants for a future career, a general liberal arts education may be the best solution.

Once a student has some idea of what he wants from college, he then can use that insight while researching colleges. Colleges and universities come in a bewildering assortment of shapes and sizes. Some have tens of thousands of students, while others have a student body of less than one thousand. In some colleges, churches or religious institutions play a dominant role in the curriculum and campus life. Some colleges are single-sex or cater to African Americans or other ethnic groups. Some institutions emphasize business or science; others, the liberal arts. Some are located in major cities; others, in the middle of the country. Some universities, including "Ivy League" institutions such as Yale and Harvard, are considered to be very prestigious; competition for admission to these elite institutions can be fierce. Less well-known colleges are often easier to get into and in many respects provide an equally good education.

High school students should read college guidebooks and catalogs, utilize online information, talk to college students they know, and visit campuses. Important questions to consider include what courses of study colleges offer, how well the school is equipped, teaching methods and class size, the school's location and accreditation, and its social environment. By November of one's senior year, Mitchell writes, "students ought to narrow the list to six to eight schools. The applicant should be able to answer yes to these questions: Will I be happy and productive at this college? And do I have a reasonable chance of getting in."

The third step—the application process—is important because the college decision is not just about high school students deciding between colleges, but colleges deciding between high school students. Colleges make decisions on acceptance and rejection based on communication with students, Mitchell argues, which is done through applications (especially the college essay), through contacts between students and college admissions officers, and via intermediaries including parents, teachers, and guidance counselors. "The application provides the primary opportunity for students to distinguish themselves," writes Mitchell. "College admissions officers seek reasons to select one qualified student over another. It's up to a student to provide them with those reasons."

Financial and Family Concerns

Money concerns are an inevitable part of the college decision. For the 2000–2001 academic year, annual prices for undergraduate tuition, room, and board were estimated to be $7,621 at public colleges and $21,423 at private colleges, according to the National Center for Education Statistics. A college education can be one of the single biggest investments anyone makes. Few students (and their families) pay the entire "sticker price" of college, however. More than 60 percent of students at four-year public colleges and universities receive some form of financial aid. That number rises to more than 75 percent of students at private colleges. Many students who apply for financial aid receive a combination of school scholarships and government grants and loans to cover costs. Factoring in how much the student and family wishes to pay (and how much debt the student wants to take on) is part of the college decision process.

Parents and family members are another inevitable part of the decision process, in part because of the financial burden they bear. The role parents play can vary. In some families, college is expected of teens; a decision to forego college could lead to major family conflict. In other families, college is not considered important and may be discouraged.

Even in cases where parents are supportive and mean the best for their teen offspring, their role in the college decision can have negative as well as positive aspects. A parent can point out college alternatives that might otherwise go unnoticed or help students focus on factors they might otherwise not consider. But parents may also attempt to choose a college for their children. Disagreement over where (and whether) to attend college can lead to family conflict. "Parents of high school seniors often believe that the college application process is their last chance to exert control over their kids' lives," writes education consultant Ted Sutton. But "for the most part, parents' instincts are dead wrong." He and others argue that while family concerns are important, it is also imperative that teens be able to focus on what is best for themselves.

The Community College Option

Some observers argue that too many students attend four-year schools without considering whether they are right for them. According to a report from the Ferris State University Career Institute for Education and Workforce Development, "This high percentage of young people planning to go to college might sound appealing, but the reality of the situation is less so. In truth, significantly fewer high-school graduates enter college, and only a fraction of those emerge with that coveted bachelor's degree. . . . The fact remains that many colleges and universities are poorly equipped to assist students who are undecided on a career."

Community colleges, or junior colleges, are an option that many teens may overlook. These two-year institutions generally cost much less than four-year colleges and offer a variety of vocational and educational options (including transferring to a four-year institution). More than 10 million students are enrolled in such institutions, the majority of whom are over twenty-two years of age. Some go to community colleges or specialized trade schools to learn specific skills in specialized fields, including culinary arts, cosmetology, health care, and electronics. Other students use community college as an inexpensive gateway to a four-year degree. Community colleges can often be a good option for those who are undecided on a major field of study and who use them to fulfill general education requirements. What can be missing from community colleges is the experience of living in residential dorms with other students.

Important Decisions

From the time students enter high school and decide which math classes to enroll in to the time they decide which college to commit the next years of their lives, the teen years can be pivotal in shaping a person's education and life. The articles and essays in *Teen Decision: Education and College* are not intended to be the first and last word on schools, but they may help you explore the options you have and the decisions you need to make to shape your own education path. In chapter 1, "Surviving High School," teachers and students discuss how to get the most out of high school and the potential risks of dropping out. Chapter 2, "Choosing a College," features articles and opinions on what kind of college may be right for you. In chapter 3, "The Admissions Game," journalists, admissions counselors, and high school students write about the process of convincing the college of your choice that you are *their* right choice. Chapter 4, "Alternatives to the Four-Year College," explores various education alternatives, including apprenticeships and the military. It is hoped that the readings in *Teen Decisions: Education and College* will inspire students to embark on more research and exploration in order to make informed choices about their education.

Chapter 1

Surviving
High School

Tips from the High School Trenches

Efrat Hakak

High school can be exciting, miserable, or both. For Efrat Hakak, her first year of high school surrounded by strangers was dismal, but she eventually succeeded in both making friends and completing high school. She shares tips on how she was able to turn high school into a positive experience in the following selection. After graduating, Hakak worked as an intern for Wholefamily.com, an online family and teen advice website.

My first day of high school was probably the worst day of my life.

My parents were forcing me to attend a prep school 45 minutes from my home. Out of a class of 110 incoming freshmen, I knew no one. Not a single person.

I had spent the last eight years in a class with 30 kids; I had not had to make a new friend at school since the first grade.

I don't think I have ever felt as lonely as I did that day, before or since.

So of course I entered school that first day with a massive chip on my shoulder. I was determined to show my parents what a stupid decision they had made.

Instead, I just depressed myself.

I joined after-school clubs, I made acquaintances; but I couldn't make any friends. I was one of those people that everybody says hello to, and even invites to sit with them at lunch, but would never call on the phone, or go out with after school.

On top of social problems, this high school was academically challenging, while my junior-high was a breeze.

> As miserable as I was that first year, the rest of high school was a blast!

After a full year of this, I was utterly miserable.

Resolutions

So I spent the summer making a few resolutions.

Maybe they can help some other people—they certainly helped me and by the end of my four years of high school, I had formed my group of friends, with whom I still keep in touch. I was even voted by the students of my class to speak at graduation. As miserable as I was that first year, the rest of high school was a blast!

Here are my resolutions:

Say hello anytime I see an acquaintance.

Because I was always smiling and greeting the people I knew, people automatically assumed I was friendly (though I am not naturally sociable). And high school kids want to be friends with sociable people.

Take the first step.

All the girls there already knew each other—they didn't need another friend. But I did, so I had to make the effort. I had to be the first one to invite somebody to go with me to a movie, or over to my house. Once I did, they started to respond in kind.

Make friends slowly.

I couldn't get discouraged when it took a while to make friends. Hey, I had already waited an entire year, what's a couple more months? Making new friends is hard.

Use classes to get to know people.

I met most of my first friends because I sat next to them in class. Class (before, after, or even during class-time!) is a great opportunity to strike up a conversation, ask for homework help, or even better, to extend help when needed.

Hide my fear.

I was terrified coming back to school sophomore year. But acting confident really helped. First of all, acting confident actually made me confident. And second, confidence implies a lack of concern for other people's opinion, which paradoxically, makes others value your opinion more. High school kids are odd in that way.

Above all, remember that it can and will get better. You may have to work a little to make your high school experience a great one, but it's absolutely worth it!

Surviving and Thriving in High School

Melissa M. Ezarik

In this article, Melissa M. Ezarik compares high school to the television show *Survivor*, in which contestants on a deserted island attempt to "Outwit, Outplay, and Outlast" each other. She argues that the requirements for winning *Survivor* and "surviving" high school are not that different, and offers suggestions on how students can learn, improve their grades, take tests, manage stress, and set priorities. Ezarik has written for *Career World* and other publications for young people.

"Reality TV" may be entertaining, but actually how real is it? If you are like the majority of teens, your life is so hectic that you may wish you were stranded on a desert island, teamed with your fellow island dwellers while you strive to outlast them.

On the show *Survivor*, the challenge is to "Outwit, Outplay, Outlast." In school, the requirements aren't much different: Use wit to succeed in class and manage to enjoy life while juggling all your roles (student, friend, family member, employee, etc.), and the lasting rewards will outweigh even a hefty reality TV show prize.

The major survival skills you need right now are academic and coping skills. On the academic side, the name of the game is grades, and study and test-taking skills are along the path to take. For coping or stress-management skills, the keys are setting priorities and realistic goals and finding ways to relax.

As you deal with the tough parts of school, you may find yourself longing for graduation. Fortunately, the skills that help you survive school are the same ones you will need throughout your work life.

Read on for a crash course in survival skills.

Outwit: Study Tips

1. Plan your time and get organized. Use a daily planner to record test dates, paper due dates, times you plan to study, and anything else that is important in your life. Schedule more time for classes that you find difficult, those that have a lot of assignments, and those with a demanding teacher.

Keep your homework space organized, too. Would you be able to find a quiet, uncluttered place to study right now? Or would you have to spend 15 minutes clearing off your desk? Make room to store school supplies and old tests and notes you don't need at the moment.

Planning and organizing are essential on the job too. If your boss asks you for the sales report for last December, you'll know where you filed it. If you are handed an unexpected rush job, you should be able to adjust your schedule to fit it in.

> The major survival skills you need right now are academic and coping skills.

Survivor tips:

"I achieve good grades in school because I write down all of my assignments in an agenda," says Chrissy, 14, who lives in Grand Rapids, Michigan. "When I am ready to go home, I look in my agenda to make sure I have all of the books that I need."

Kody, 17, from Sandy, Utah, suggests, "Get a separate folder for each class and keep it organized." That way, you won't waste your study time searching for materials from a certain class.

2. *Keep on top of your assignments.* If you do, you won't be learning the material for the first time when you start studying for a test. Dr. Carolyn Hopper, a professor at Middle Tennessee State University and the author of *Practicing College Study Skills*, suggests that students "prepare for each class as if there will be a pop quiz." Keep up with the reading and get an early start on your projects. Being prepared each day will help you get the most out of each class period. And you will avoid the panic of having too much to do in too little time at the end of the term.

> Taking good notes during class is essential.

What should you do when your teacher doesn't check homework? It's easy to skip it when time is tight, but consider sharing your efforts instead. Compare answers with your classmates. If you don't agree on an answer, ask the teacher to go over it.

3. *Learn to take good notes.* Taking good notes during class is essential. Write down as much as you can, paying attention to clues about what's important. For example, teachers often write main ideas down on the board, start off a statement by saying it's important, or speak more slowly when giving facts you'll need to know. Dr. Hopper points out that you can take notes faster if you don't use complete sentences and if you abbreviate wherever possible. You might even try inventing your own abbreviations for words you use often. Also, look over your notes after class to see if you have any questions and to mark the important parts.

When taking notes at home, try to identify the main idea of each chapter, and then check to see what your teacher emphasized in class. Try to concentrate on those parts. Never copy full sentences from the book—always summarize in your own words.

In the workplace, you may need to take notes or summarize important information. If you have to learn to use a new computer program to access your work files, you will know what steps to take if you made a note. If your supervisor asks you to summarize the important points of a report for your co-workers, you will know how to do it effectively.

Survivor tips:

Katherine, 15, from Shirley, New York, suggests, "Get a recorder and bring it to school and record the teacher. . . . If there is something important that you need to study for, you have it in the palm of your hand."

Jenn, 17, of New York City, offers these tips on taking notes from a textbook: "I color-code them and make sure that every fact that could possibly be on the test is in my notes."

4. Stay focused and on task. Getting down to business for studying is no easy job. Suddenly, everything from cleaning your room to giving the dog a bath can seem like more fun.

Make sure your family and friends know that you plan to study and don't want to be interrupted. Then remind yourself that the sooner you begin, the sooner you'll be done. Bob Wilson, a staff counselor at George Washington University, says, "Everybody procrastinates at one time or another, over one thing or another. The trick is knowing what you procrastinate over, how, and why." There may be a certain type of assignment you put off, or a certain time of day you tend to procrastinate. Also be conscious of what you tend to do instead. Unplug the TV or computer, turn on the answering machine, or do whatever you have to do to avoid these obstacles.

> Getting down to business for studying is no easy job.

While you're studying, try to become interested in the topic. "If a subject is boring to you, find a friend who likes it and ask why," suggests Dr. Jeanne Shay Schumm in her book *School Power.* "Read a magazine article, watch a video about it, or surf the Internet for material on that subject."

What about daydreaming? Dr. Schumm says, "If you start to fade or daydream, stop. Stand up, stretch, jump up and down, munch an apple, or take a short nap—if you really need it."

Being focused on the task at hand, well-organized, and efficient will take you a long way toward reaching your goals at school and later in a career.

Outplay: Test-Taking Secrets

Knowledge is power when it comes to doing well on tests—but this knowledge goes beyond knowing the material.

1. *Find out as much as you can about the test from your teacher.*

Ask these types of questions:

- Will the test cover everything from the whole year, or just information since the last test?
- What format will it be (multiple choice, short answer, essay, etc.)? If it's more than one format, what parts will be worth the most points?
- Will the test take the whole class period?
- Are we allowed to bring anything (such as a note card with formulas or a calculator for math class)? Your teacher might have even forgotten to mention that it's an open-book test!

Don't be embarrassed about asking these questions—chances are, almost everyone else wants to know, too.

If your teacher offers to spend class time reviewing before a test, always come prepared with questions. He or she may move on to new material if no one asks anything.

> Knowledge is power when it comes to doing well on tests.

Survivor tips:

"I'm kind of quiet, so whenever I have a question for a teacher, I turn to someone near me who is outgoing," says Lisa, 18, of Storrs, Connecticut. "I ask, 'What do you think will be on this test?' And it never fails—he'll turn toward the teacher and ask the question himself."

Matt, 16, of Stanford, Connecticut, offers this advice: "If your teacher says something more than once, it's going to be on a test.

And if he tells you to write it down, it's going to be on a test."

2. *Use what you've learned about the test.* Here are some tips for studying for certain types of tests:

- Flash cards are ideal for tests when you have to know the meanings of terms.
- When trying to remember important names and dates, try making a timeline or composing a song or poem.
- For essay tests, Dr. Schumm suggests thinking up some possible questions and writing what you would say. Then go over your essays "with a teacher's eye." How could they be better? What have you forgotten?

3. *Form a study group to teach others about the material you're comfortable with and to get help with what you're not.* Remember that study groups aren't a substitute for studying on your own. Each member should prepare ahead of time. Here are some rules for running an effective study group:

> While it probably ranks as the most stressful, school is just one aspect of your life.

- Have an agenda. What material do you need to cover? Each member can choose a section to concentrate on before the group meets.
- Take turns "presenting" each of your sections to the group. Then quiz the group on some practice questions. Finally, everyone can brainstorm other questions that might come up on the test.

4. *Do your best during the test.* After all of your hard work, you don't want nerves to take over on test day. Here's how to get through the experience:

- It sounds simple, but don't forget to read the directions carefully. What may look like a standard true-false section, for instance, might actually call for changing false statements to make them true.
- "Do a mind dump," says Dr. Hopper, after you've read through the test. "Make notes of anything you think you

might forget. Write down things that you used in learning the material that might help you remember."

- Answer the easy questions first, Dr. Hopper says. "This will give you the confidence and momentum to get through the rest of the test."
- Look over the test after you've finished. Many test-taking experts say that your first instinct is usually best. But a study of more than 1,000 students by a University of Michigan professor found that answers were changed from wrong to right 2.5 times more often than they were changed from right to wrong.
- For essays, first create a mini-outline. It will help keep your thoughts organized; and if you run out of time, your teacher may give you partial credit.
- In multiple choice tests, the answer "all of the above" is often the correct one, says Dr. Hopper. For true-false tests, don't assume the answer is false unless you know it is—true is usually a better guess.
- Ignore classmates who finish before you. "It's a myth that top students finish first," says Dr. Schumm.

Being a committed learner and taking responsibility for your own learning are important parts of being successful—not only in school, but also at work. Employers appreciate employees who learn willingly and expand their job skills.

Outlast: Coping Clues

While it probably ranks as the most stressful, school is just one aspect of your life. And sometimes life spins out of control. How do you fit in all of your commitments and interests? Take note of the following stress-management tips:

1. Prioritize your life. Donald Martin, author of the book *How to Be a Successful Student*, advocates using a "3-List Method":

- Use a weekly calendar. List everything from study time and work to relaxation time. "Keep your schedule handy and refer to it often," he says. "If it doesn't work, change it."

- Write down "things to do" each day. Write down everything you want and need to do for the day. You can refer to it and decide what is most important.
- Set goals. What do you want to accomplish over the next month or year? This list can help you to "develop long-term goals and to free your mind to concentrate on today," Martin says.

If ranking your to-do list is difficult, Wilson suggests asking yourself which activities are both important and urgent. Also, he believes that "truly important tasks require a timeline from the due date, working back to the start."

Check yourself throughout the day to see if you're using your time wisely. Everybody needs time to relax, but spending hours each day just hanging out is too much.

> Setting priorities, organizing your time, and simply relaxing are strategies that will help you cope throughout your life.

Survivor tips:

Lou, 18, of Milford, Connecticut, says a to-do list "keeps you in line and helps you get your priorities straight."

"I think about the long-term effects of each activity, and I do the ones that will play the biggest factor in my future," says Kody, 17, of Sandy, Utah.

2. *Set realistic goals.* According to Dr. Hopper, a useful goal has five elements: It is specific, measurable, challenging, realistic, and achievable by a certain date. An example: "My goal is to improve my English grade from a C to a B by next semester."

Breaking your goal into several smaller steps with deadlines of their own can make achieving it more manageable. To improve your English grade, think of every homework assignment, test, and paper as a mini-deadline and another chance to move closer to the goal.

Survivor tips:

Noeleen, 14, from Philadelphia, decided she wanted to be

ranked first in her class. "I have to do well throughout the whole year," she told herself. After dedicating herself to her studies, Noeleen reached her goal.

Katherine, 15, from Shirley, New York, wants to become a professional singer someday, which she realizes will not be easy. "I am already working on it by writing record companies and sending tapes," she says.

3. Find ways to relax. Research shows that stress doesn't affect people as much when they have friends and family to lean on. Whether it's talking to friends online, going out with friends, or spending time with your pet, turning to a loved one helps when you're stressed. Other popular ways to relax include the following:

- Listening to music or playing an instrument
- Working out or playing a sport
- Writing or drawing
- Taking a bath
- Spending time outside
- Sleeping! What feels like stress could just be exhaustion.

Setting priorities, organizing your time, and simply relaxing are strategies that will help you cope throughout your life. If your boss asks you to stay late on a Friday to help manage a crisis, for example, you should take a deep breath, adjust your after-work plans, and pitch in where you're needed.

With all of the skills described above, you will find that surviving school gets a whole lot easier. Keep in mind the rules of how to "Outwit, Outplay, and Outlast." Your reality, now and in the future, will be success!

How to Build a Strong Academic Record

American Federation of Teachers

Among the choices students make in high school is what courses to take. The decisions they make can determine what future they will have after high school. The following selection, taken from a publication by the American Federation of Teachers (AFT), stresses the importance of building a strong academic record that will enable students to be accepted in colleges and avoid being stuck in minimum-wage jobs. Using a question-and-answer format, the AFT argues that students should take challenging courses, including mathematics and a foreign language, with an eye toward their academic future. It is better to get an occasional B or a C in an advanced course than straight A's in easy classes. The AFT is the nation's second-largest labor organization representing teachers and other education workers.

It's worth repeating: Your high school academic record is the single most important thing colleges consider when deciding who to accept. So, how do you get a good one? The answer is: Take challenging academic courses and work hard to get good grades. Here are the longer answers to some common questions.

American Federation of Teachers, *Hard Work Pays*, 1999. Copyright © 1999 by American Federation of Teachers. Reproduced by permission. Entire article can be found on AFT's website: www.aft.org/reports/index.html.

What Kinds of Courses Should I Take in High School?

When you enter high school, you'll probably face many choices about what courses to take. Taking easy courses so you can "get by" is always the wrong choice. It may be tempting to take easy courses. This way, you can sail through high school and have more time to hang out with friends. But let's get real: Getting into college is competitive. Colleges don't want students with a "get-by" education when they know they can have their pick.

To build a strong high school academic record, you need to take challenging courses in subjects such as math, English, science, history, and a foreign language. You may want to take additional courses based on your interests, but these are the main courses colleges want you to take.

Taking challenging courses in math, English, science, history, and a foreign language will pay off. Students who take such courses and work hard do better in high school, score higher on standardized tests, and get into better colleges. Taking these courses will also help you build the basic skills that you are going to use all of your life, no matter what you do for a living.

You might be thinking: "This doesn't make any sense. If I take easy courses, at least I can get all A's. And isn't that what colleges want to see?" Wrong! If you remember one thing from [reading] this, remember this: Good colleges would much rather accept a student who gets straight B's (and even an occasional C) in challenging courses than a student who gets straight A's in easy courses.

> Taking easy courses so you can "get by" is always the wrong choice.

What Are Some Examples of "Challenging" Courses?

You may be thinking: "Math, English, science, history, and a foreign language. I'm starting to get the picture. But there are lots of courses that have 'math' or 'English' or 'science' in the title. How do I know which courses are the challenging ones that colleges want me to take?"

Good question. The answer depends a lot on the courses your school offers. That's why it's smart to talk to a teacher or guidance counselor before you choose courses. If possible, do this even before you start high school. Tell a counselor or teacher that you want to take challenging academic courses (often called "college prep" courses) because you are serious about doing well in high school and going to college—even if it means getting a little extra help to catch up. If a guidance counselor or teacher is not immediately available, don't give up. Be a pest, if you have to, until you get the help you need.

> It's smart to talk to a teacher or guidance counselor before you choose courses.

Hints on Choosing Classes

As you sit down with teachers, guidance counselors, and other trusted adults to pick the right courses, keep in mind these helpful hints:

Try to take algebra and geometry as soon as possible—preferably by the end of the eighth and ninth grades. It's a fact: Students who take algebra and geometry early on are much more likely to go to college than students who don't. One reason is that you generally must take algebra and geometry before you can take advanced math and science courses such as trigonometry, calculus, chemistry, and physics. And these advanced courses are exactly the kinds of courses colleges want you to take.

Consider learning a foreign language as soon as possible—preferably before you start high school. The longer you study a foreign language, the more interested colleges will be in you. Many colleges require students to study at least two years of the same foreign language, and just about all of them prefer as many years as possible. Studying a foreign language has other benefits, too. It will increase your verbal skills, which could mean a higher SAT I or ACT score. It will show your future employers that you're ready to compete in the "global economy," increasing your chances of landing an exciting job that involves travel to faraway places. And it will deepen your understanding of other people and ways of life. Wouldn't it be fun to visit a country such as Mexico, Spain, France, Russia, or Japan and be able to speak their language?

Advanced Courses

Once you start high school, ask about the specific courses listed in the [following] table. Students who take challenging courses such as these and work hard at them do better in high school, score higher on standardized tests, and get into better colleges. Some colleges require many of these courses. Contact the colleges you're interested in to find out. Ask about higher-level courses. Many high schools offer Advanced Placement (AP), International Baccalaureate (IB), Honors, Gifted, or Enrichment programs. If your high school does, see what you have to do to get into one of these programs. Because these programs tend to be very challenging, students who participate in them have an even better chance of going on to good colleges and getting good jobs.

Recommended High School Coursework

Subjects	Math	English	Lab Science	History	Foreign Language	Arts	Electives
Number of Years	4	4	3	3	3 (in the same language)	1–3	1–3
Types of Courses	Algebra I	Composition	Earth Science	U.S. History	Spanish	Art	Computer Sci.
	Geometry	American Lit.	Geology	European History	French	Dance	Statistics
	Algebra II	English Lit.	Biology		German	Drama	Economics
	Trigonometry	World Lit.	Chemistry	World History	Latin	Music	Psychology
	Pre-Calculus		Physics	U.S. Government	Russian		Communications
	Calculus			Geography	Japanese		
				Civics			

Avoid courses in the general track. Such courses might include "general math," or "general science." Courses in the general track are often less challenging than the courses listed in the table. Remember: Colleges want you to take the most challenging courses that are offered at your school.

Do I Really Need to Take Challenging Courses in All Subjects?

You may be thinking: "Okay, I'll take challenging courses, but just not in math. I hate math, and I'll never use it anyway. Besides, if I take easy math courses, then I can concentrate on the subjects that I am good at." It's natural to want to take courses in subjects that you like and do well in. It's fun, and it makes you feel good about yourself. And over time, you'll probably want to focus more on the subjects you like.

> Consider learning a foreign language as soon as possible.

But it's also important to take courses in areas that you are not necessarily that good at or interested in—at least not yet. Why? The biggest reason is that colleges like to see academic achievement in many subjects. In fact, most colleges would rather accept a student who is solid (but not great) in many areas than one who is great in one area but bad in all the rest. Another reason is that your interests might change, just as your tastes in foods or music or clothes will undoubtedly change. There's so much to learn out there that it's simply too early to rule anything out.

What If I Don't Want to Go to College Right After High School?

So far, [we have] mainly talked about what you need to do to prepare for a four-year college or university, where you would earn what's called a "bachelor's degree." We've done so because, for the most part, people who finish four years of college have more job opportunities and earn more money than people who don't.

Vocational Programs

However, if you feel that you won't be ready for a four-year college right after high school, you still have many options. For example, many high schools offer "vocational" or "technical" programs that train you for careers after high school in a particular field. One good option you may want to ask a teacher or guidance counselor about is a vocational program with ties to a local two-year "junior," "community," or "technical" college. These programs, often called "tech-prep," "2+2," or "school-to-career," allow you to continue your career training at a two-year college until you earn what's called an "associate's degree."

What are some of the benefits of having an associate's degree? Although associate's degree graduates, in general, have fewer career options than bachelor's degree graduates, associate's de-

> The sad part is that students who believe they are "dumb" usually do poorly in school.

gree graduates are often able to land high-paying jobs in fields they enjoy. For example, the following are just a few of the jobs open to associate's degree graduates: computer technician, nurse, commercial artist, medical assistant, executive secretary, hotel/restaurant manager, and auto mechanic.

And here's another big benefit of having an associate's degree: If you decide later in life that you want to continue your education, many four-year colleges will accept an associate's degree as credit toward a bachelor's degree. This means, for example, that you may only have to go to college for another two years before earning a bachelor's degree.

Just remember: If you are considering a vocational program that prepares you for work right after high school or for more training at a two-year college, make sure the program is a good one. Some vocational programs teach very narrow skills that end up being outdated by the time you graduate. This makes it hard to find a job.

How can you tell if a vocational program is a good one? Here are some questions you might want to ask a teacher or guidance counselor:

- Do students in the vocational program finish high school,

or do most of them drop out?

- Do students in the vocational program take the kinds of challenging academic courses that a college would accept?
- Do students in the vocational program later go on to two- or four-year colleges?
- Do students in the vocational program eventually land good, high-paying jobs in their field, or do most end up working for minimum wage—for example, flipping burgers?

Am I Really Smart Enough?

You might be thinking: "I would like to take challenging courses, but I'm just not smart enough. Tough courses are for the bright kids, not me." The sad part is that students who believe they are "dumb" usually do poorly in school. On the other hand, most students who believe they can achieve do achieve. It's not magic. It's because if you believe you can achieve, you make it your business to do that.

Success Takes Hard Work

Any person who has made it would say the same: Success doesn't just come "naturally." It takes hard work. This is true no matter what you do in life. Just think for a second about your favorite professional athletes. If basketball is their game, do you think they were ready to play in the NBA or WNBA the first time they stepped onto a court? Or your favorite musicians. If they sing, how many sour notes do you think they hit before being good enough to perform in front of thousands of people? Or your favorite movie stars. How many small roles do you think they were forced to take before getting their big break?

Doing well in school is no different from doing well in sports, music, the arts, or any other activity.

Or think about your own life. Remember the first time you drew a picture, threw a football, performed in a play, or tried a musical instrument. Pretty embarrassing, right? But with practice and coaching, you got better. Doing well in school is no different from doing well in sports, music, the arts, or any other activity. It takes time, effort, and determination. This means participating in classroom lessons, completing homework assignments, and studying for tests and quizzes.

Because you will be taking challenging courses, doing well won't always be easy. For example, if you study Shakespeare's plays in English class, you may need to read a passage from *Romeo and Juliet* two or three times before you understand it. Or, you might not be able to solve a tough geometry problem the first time around. The key is not to let a few setbacks stop you from going after what you want. Everyone struggles with Shakespeare and geometry. And, as you'll see soon, there are people out there who can help you when you need a boost.

Think about it this way. Who do you have more respect for: a track-and-field high jumper who sets the bar a foot off the ground and clears it every time or a jumper who sets the bar six feet off the ground and misses it by inches on his first attempt but clears it on his second or third?

Okay. I Get Your Point. But Where Can I Get Extra Help If I Need It?

If you feel you may be slipping behind in your studies, there are many people out there who can and want to help you. They may include:

Family members. Talk to a parent, grandparent, aunt, uncle, or older sibling. Who knows? You may discover a math whiz in your own family. And even if family members can't help you do your algebra homework, they may be able to help you find someone who can.

Adults at your school. Talk to a teacher, guidance counselor, librarian, or principal. Ask them if they know of any before-school, after-school, or summer school "extra help" or tutoring programs. You may also want to ask about special "mentor" programs. Through a mentor program, you are paired with a college student or graduate who can help you with your studies and give you advice on how to plan for college.

Adults in your community. Talk to trusted adults at your local library, church or synagogue, youth center (such as the YMCA/YWCA, or Boys/Girls Club), or community group (such as the NAACP or Urban League). These places often run after-school programs and other activities.

Friends. Think about forming study groups with your friends, especially the ones who are also serious about going to college. Not only does group learning help, it can be a lot more fun.

Sometimes, you'll get help the first time you ask for it. Other times, help may not be immediately available. If this is the case, we remind you again: Don't give up. . . .

Yes, a good education is going to take some sweat—maybe even some tears. But of all the things that you could invest in— from CDs to clothes to cars—can you think of anything more valuable than your mind? CDs scratch. Clothes go out of style. Cars stop running. Your mind is the only thing that you're going to have all your life. You better make sure that it works.

The Consequences of "Senioritis"

Jennifer Mrozowski

Many high school seniors lose motivation to work hard or keep up with their classwork. Jennifer Mrozowski, a journalist for the *Cincinnati Enquirer*, examines this phenomenon, sometimes jokingly called "senioritis." She reports that some students lose interest in school after being accepted to college, while others are too busy juggling jobs and other activities. A serious case of "senioritis" could result in the rescission of college acceptance or scholarships, she writes.

Senior slack. Senior slump. Senioritis. The terminology may sound cute, but it masks a malady that some local educators say is striking earlier and more often in high school. Too many students are coasting through their senior years, apparently spending more time working and partying and less time studying.

The consequences can be serious:

- Nearly one-third of students entering college require remedial help.
- Colleges can revoke admissions and scholarships.

"I started experiencing ('senioritis') in the first couple weeks of school," said Anderson High School senior David Rosenfeldt, 17.

"You lose all your motivation to study and do homework. When you get accepted into college, it's hard to keep your concentration."

Kings High School senior Lindsay Woods, 17, also pleaded guilty.

"After applying to colleges and getting accepted, you don't care about grades anymore." Lindsay, an A-range student, has already been accepted to several of the schools to which she applied.

Finishing every written assignment and completing all the required reading is a challenge, she said.

"You're so exhausted by your senior year—you're just tired of doing it," Lindsay said. "Plus, you want to experience as much socially as you can."

> Nearly one-third of students entering college require remedial help.

A report released last month [January 2001] by the National Commission on the High School Senior Year painted a dismal picture of the state of high schools, saying many parents and students don't know what it takes to succeed in postsecondary education. Even high-achieving students drift through their senior year, treating it as a "prolonged farewell to adolescence," the report's authors said.

The commission, chaired by Kentucky Gov. Paul Patton, is made up of teachers, school administrators, business leaders and legislators.

At Raymond Walters College in Blue Ash, remediation is a problem, said Mary Stagaman, director of college relations at the two-year campus for the University of Cincinnati.

About a third of incoming freshmen at Ohio's two-year colleges require remediation, she said.

"I think 30 percent is a matter of concern," Ms. Stagaman

said. "The faculty here working to reduce remediation would say we have a way to go."

Juggling Activities

Work outside school can be a major problem, according to a 1998 report by the National Research Council and the Institute of Medicine—two divisions of the National Academy of Sciences.

Students under 18 who work more than 20 hours per week don't do as well in school, according to the report. They're also more likely to use drugs and forsake sleep and exercise.

About 44 percent of 16- and 17-year-olds work at some point throughout the year, either while in school or during the summer, according to the Labor Department. But in surveys of high school students, about 80 percent say they held a job during the school year at some point in high school.

Laura Curtin, 17, an A student at Beechwood High School in Fort Mitchell, said she sacrifices sleep for her after-school job at the Fort Mitchell Drug Shoppe.

Laura works 20 to 25 hours a week, often 3:30-to-9 P.M. shifts on weekdays, to pay for car insurance. She may skip softball this spring because she would have to find substitutes at work.

"Sometimes (work) does get in the way," Laura said. "Getting schoolwork done can be a balancing act of late nights and pre-planning."

Not all students balance as well.

"If students try to work too many hours, do too many extracurricular activities and study, something's going to suffer," said Dr. Fred Bassett, superintendent of the Beechwood Independent School District.

> Work outside school can be a major problem.

Campbell County High School principal Stephen Sorrell, an educator of 20-plus years, said "senioritis" strikes earlier every year.

"Kids are seeing an end to a section of their lives and are ready to move on," Mr. Sorrell said. "The best thing we can do is keep them interested in what they're learning."

Ashley Oltman, a mostly A student at Kings, said she scheduled fun classes her final semester—art and photography—in part to maintain her interest.

Ashley has had a busy year, working three days a week, serving as president of her church's youth group, participating in the school curriculum council and taking a sign language class.

"This keeps my mind focused on something," she said as she assembled a photo collage in a recent class. "I have a fun project to do, not like a book report."

Colleges Do Watch

Colleges and universities can rescind acceptance or scholarships if a student fails miserably his senior year.

Jody Petersen, a guidance counselor at Cincinnati Hills Christian Academy, said she tells students that colleges pay attention to grades from day one of freshman year to the last day of senior year.

Patrick Herring, director of Undergraduate Admission at the University of Kentucky, said he also pays close attention to high school seniors' course loads. Blow-off years don't bode well for acceptance there, he said.

Seniors have better chances if they take at least four academic classes in their final high school year, he said, with two being advanced-placement classes—those are classes in which college credit can be received.

"We tell them the senior year schedule can make all the difference in the world," he said.

Why You Should Stay in School

Julianne Dueber

Julianne Dueber is a former high school teacher and author of *The Ultimate High School Survival Guide.* In the following excerpt from that book, Dueber provides reasons why students, even those who are struggling, should not drop out of high school. She argues that high school dropouts face much worse job prospects than do high school and college graduates. Furthermore, graduating from high school will earn you more respect both from others and yourself. Many communities have alternatives to regular public high schools for obtaining a high school education, including alternative schools, correspondence courses, and summer schools. In addition, people who have not finished high school can take a test and receive a General Educational Development (GED) certificate.

Do you want to flip burgers the rest of your life? You will not be using your mind as well as you could if you stayed in school and got your education. Plus, by flipping burgers, you're constantly standing on your feet. Feet need a rest too. Give them a break. Stay in school and sit a spell.

High school dropouts earn much less than high school and college graduates. Check out the average hourly wage and annual salary of the following professions.

Profession	Hourly Wage	Annual Wage	Training Required
1			
Cashier	$6.96	$14,480	None
Waitress	$5.87	$12,200	None
Cook (fast food)	$6.11	$12,700	None
Baggage porter/bellhop	$6.92	$14,400	None
Parking lot attendant	$7.06	$14,680	None
2			
Heating, air conditioning and refrigeration mechanic	$14.48	$30,120	High school diploma or associate's degree
Fire inspector	$20.36	$42,340	High school diploma or associate's degree
Aircraft mechanic	$17.65	$36,710	High school diploma or associate's degree
3			
Financial manager	$27.43	$57,060	High school diploma
General manager	$29.31	$60,960	4-year college
Education administrator	$26.87	$55,900	Some graduate work
Management analyst	$25.05	$52,110	Some graduate work

Information gathered from the Bureau of Labor Statistics of the U.S. Department of Labor, 1997, the latest figures available when this book went to press. . . .

List 1 includes the type of jobs for which high school dropouts qualify. These are the jobs you will be doing if you do not finish high school.

List 2 includes jobs you can do with a high school diploma and additional training, either through trade school or an employer training program. No employer will consider training you for a career if you don't have that high school degree.

List 3 includes jobs for which you must have a college degree.

Notice the huge salary difference when you get a college degree. It makes a big difference to get more education. It pays to hang in there and keep on going. Some day you will be very glad you did.

Consider the Consequences

Fast food jobs are survival-only jobs. You will have to work overtime hours to pay all of your bills. Minimum wage jobs are dead-end jobs. If you are thinking of dropping out of high school, consider the consequences.

Higher education pays off big time. With your high school education and training after high school, you will be able to take better care of your future family. You will have enough extra money to travel and do the things you enjoy. You don't want to have to live with your parents because you can't afford to live on your own, do you? You need to graduate from high school, then get some training or a college education. That's just a fact of life.

You want some self-respect. If you drop out now, you will always regret it when you're older. People will not treat you with as much respect as they do people with more education. I have talked to numerous people who did not continue their education after high school and they all regret not going on to trade school or college.

70 to 80 percent of criminals are high school dropouts. Because they are having a hard time paying their bills, they turn to crime to feed themselves and their families. Don't become a part of this tragic statistic.

> High school dropouts earn much less than high school and college graduates.

High school graduates, on the average, earn $6415 more per year than high school dropouts. Information gathered from the Bureau of the Census, 1994. . . .

Students from low-income families are 2.4 times more likely to drop out of school than are children from middle-income fam-

ilies, and 10.5 times more likely than students from high-income families. Information gathered from the U.S. Department of Commerce, Economics and Statistics Administration, 1993. . . .

Other Options Besides Your High School

Some of you will have a hard time surviving in a regular public high school. When you think that there is no way for you to be successful, you might turn to cutting classes, doing drugs, or just drop out. If you find yourself in this situation and you have truly tried your hardest to do well but you just seem to keep getting into trouble, talk to your counselor about other options. Here are some of the things you can do instead of attending your regular public high school:

> If you drop out now, you will always regret it when you're older.

Some larger districts have magnet schools. If you live in a large school district that has magnet schools, call up the administrative office to check out what the requirements are for admission. Often, these schools have special schools for the arts, music, or technology. They can be a great option for students who are unhappy with their public high school.

Many districts have alternative schools for students who fail to succeed in the regular public high school. Ask your counselor if you can transfer. She will help you if she feels you need to make a change.

Summer school helps you get back on track. If you fail some classes and are hopelessly behind, you can catch up by taking summer school classes. It should help you to catch up with the classmates you started high school with. Do you want to be in classes with freshmen and sophomores when you should be a junior or senior?

Correspondence courses are another option. Some high schools allow you to take correspondence courses associated with your state university for credit. You have to be very motivated to work on your own, do the classwork, send it in, and take the tests. No one will be demanding that you take tests at a certain time. You alone will determine whether you pass the class.

The General Educational Development (GED) test. If you don't finish high school, you can take a test that certifies you have a high school–level knowledge of reading and writing skills and know English grammar. In addition, passing the test will show that you know as much math, social studies, and science as the typical high school graduate. When you pass the test, you will get a certificate known as the GED.

Students take the GED for many reasons. Some may be very bright and feel that high school is a waste of their time. Others take it because they had problems with drugs and alcohol in high school and either dropped out or failed. Most students who pass the GED go on to a community college. Another option is to get a job with an employer who will train you for a profession. Many companies are willing to give a GED-certified student a chance if he shows lots of promise and ambition. In addition, some four-year colleges accept GED students. One university I know of even has a scholarship for high-scoring GED students.

> You must never give up hope, even if you flunk several classes or drop out of high school.

You must never give up hope, even if you flunk several classes or drop out of high school. I know a boy who handcuffed himself to his bed so that he wouldn't have to go to school. He dropped out of high school, but later got his GED. He is making a good living now and has gone on to get a college degree. His grades were good, but he just hated high school. There are many routes to success and no student should *ever* feel that his life is hopeless. Never give up hope.

Experiences of a High School Dropout

Diana Moreno

Every year, hundreds of thousands of high school students drop out of school without graduating. The following article from *New Youth Connections*, a New York–based youth publication, is the autobiographical story of one high school dropout. Diana Moreno first stopped attending classes during her freshman year. Subsequent attempts to reenter high school and catch up with her friends failed. She writes about what made her drop out, her life outside of high school, and the reasons why she eventually returned and is determined to get a diploma. When she wrote this essay she was attending an alternative high school in New York City.

M y life as a drop out . . . where do I begin?

I guess you could say that I came to a fork in a road and chose to follow the wrong path to reach my goal—you know, a short cut.

I thought I had found an easy way out from the hard work I dreaded. But I learned there is no such thing as a short cut, an easy way out—you have to work hard in order to make it.

I guess that's why I'm here now telling you what dropping out of school was like for me, and why I decided to return.

I Want That Diploma

I'm in school now because I've decided that I want to have that diploma to wave around like a gold medal. I have set myself up with a goal to graduate high school—and that's what I'm going to do.

It isn't always easy, and I still think about dropping out. Sometimes I feel like I always have that white surrender flag flapping in the air and I feel like a loser and that I'm not going to make it.

But then I think of my family, the ones who always say, "I told you so," and I snap and realize I can't do that to myself. Then I crawl, I try to crawl out of that big black gaping hole that I have dug for myself.

I Was a Bookworm and a Nerd

So let me get back to the story and tell you a little about myself and my school mess up.

First off, before you read this and think, "Hell, she's one of those girls who probably never made it past junior high school without the help of the soft teachers," I just have to prove you wrong.

> I learned there is no such thing as a short cut.

Growing up, I was basically your average bookworm, or what my peers used to call me—a NERD.

I always had my hand up in class. If I passed a test, I didn't mind showing it off. Kids called me a geek because I didn't just turn in my homework, I did extra credit, too.

I liked school, and the first time I dropped out, at the start of my freshman year, it was more of an accident.

I had just moved to the Bronx to live with my mom, but I was supposed to be attending a school in Brooklyn, and the travel time was hectic. So I tried to transfer out.

My mom had all the papers, but I was told that it was too late to transfer and I would have to wait for the February term to begin.

At the time, my mom, well, she was in another world. She had her own problems to deal with. And with no one making sure I got my act together, I just let everything slide.

The Action Passed Me By

In fact, I wound up staying out of school for the whole year. I kind of enjoyed myself in the beginning. But the fun came to a halt when the warm days begun to fade.

I found myself constantly alone—everyone was moving on and I was just sitting still while the action passed me by.

I would be home doing nothing, gaining weight, lying in bed watching TV or reading, while my friends were in school, and I would hope for 3 o'clock to hurry up and come so that I could go and chill.

What's amazing is that after a few weeks I found myself craving school and wanting to make my brain bigger. I would actually go and do my friend's brother's homework.

I used to get all hyped when he told me he got an A or B plus on an assignment I did for him. At first, I didn't mind too much that he was getting credit for my work because I had a crush on him. But later I decided that he'd better do his own work, and I went back to being bored.

Scared to Go Outside

There wasn't much I could do during the day.

I was scared to go outside because I was underage and didn't want the cops to pick me up and put my mom in problems. And I didn't want to go outside because it was already starting to get cold—always looking like it was going to rain.

I didn't like going outside if no one was around—it bothered me knowing that my friends were in school while I was home slowly deteriorating.

I found myself reading books with words I'd never heard of and looking up the meanings so I'd understand and develop my vocabulary.

I liked to find ways to use my new-found knowledge in my sentences and have people comment, "Hey, you're a smart kid." But I dreaded what came next: "Then why aren't you in school?" Someone always found a way to bust my bubble.

I began to feel that my future had no real meaning unless I was in school, and I wanted to return.

"You Wasted Enough Time"

But the person who really got me back in school was my uncle. He literally dragged me from school to school trying to get me in. We went to three schools in the same day—and we were walking. I had blisters on my feet by the time I got home.

"You're going to school whether you like it or not," he raved. "You wasted enough time. If no school will take you then you're going to your zone and that's final!" The next day I was enrolled.

When I returned, I already had it in my mind that I was going to pass all of my classes and be on the honor roll and return to the kind of student I used to be.

But that only lasted one quarter of the semester. I was so used to not being in school that it was hard for me to get used to the class rules and get focused.

I started out my days saying that I was going to succeed—but I found I was behind more than I had expected.

"How Am I Going to Catch Up?"

I constantly felt like I was under water and needed some air to breathe. "How am I going to catch up?" I wondered.

What made it harder was that I was also trying to prove myself to people in my family.

See, in my family, there aren't many graduates. My mom never made it past 9th grade and she repeated it three times. My uncle Luis made it to Long Island University but never completed his course of study. Still, he, my mom and my grandma instill in me the desire for an education.

Percentage of 18- through 24-year-olds who had completed high school* (completion rate)

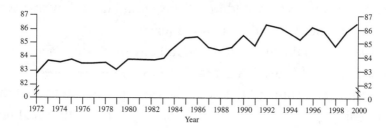

*Excludes those still enrolled in high school.

U.S. Department of Commerce, U.S. Census Bureau, Current Population Survey (CPS), October 1972–2000.

But other people in my family, like my aunt Lucy, fill me with doubt. She tells me I'm too high up on my horse and soon I'm going to fall off, and sometimes that negative talk makes it easier for me to fall.

I always said I wasn't going to be like my family, I was going to make it, but when I found school hard and began to mess up, I found myself thinking, "Oh my God, maybe I am nothing and am destined to be nothing," and that scared me.

Besides, it was easy to cut. All my friends were cutting, too.

It would be "Come on Diana—let's go chill. Come on—after today you could stop but just for today let's go do something. Come on it's only the beginning of the term—these first few days of classes don't really matter, you could make it up later," and so I was pulled in.

I Became a No Show

And at my school, anyone wanting to leave the building could just walk right on out past security.

They don't care what happens to us once we go out those doors, and actually, I don't blame them—we make our choices for ourselves. If we want to learn, we go to school—if we don't, we become no shows. Which is what I became.

By January, I found myself cutting more and more by myself. After a while, I would only show up for two or three periods (mainly so my twin wouldn't tell my grandmother, who I was living with then), and then I would leave.

Usually I would cut at least one full day of classes each week. Instead, I would just hang around, explore Sears and chill at Mickey D's when it got chilly.

> I began to feel that my future had no real meaning unless I was in school.

All that time, I didn't really see the future past the next day or week or month, and I assumed I had all the time in the world to correct my mistakes. The only time I thought about the future was when I was daydreaming.

I would daydream about my senior prom and my graduation, with my whole family there clapping and cheering, some crying that I actually made it.

Too Laid Back

But sometimes I'd blink and I'd be back to the present and it was "Oh WOW! I have a lot to accomplish and so little time to do it." And if you're like me, this is usually the time where you get stuck and shake your head like a wet dog shakes his body and say to yourself, "What am I going to do?"

But after I pulled my hair out a little, I would get laid back and tell myself, "Oh, well, no one's perfect." I would convince myself that my family couldn't be mad at me because they didn't make it anywhere themselves.

At the end of the year, when I got my final report card, I realized I only had seven credits for the whole year. I laughed at this, but I also decided again that next year I would do better. But I didn't. By November, I was already messing up.

I would go to school feeling that this time I was going to make it, then things would appear harder than they really were. I would get frustrated and search for an escape.

Your Average Couch Potato

In February, I decided to enroll in a class to get my GED in order to not have to go through the stressing ordeal of high school. But I was bored, and after about three weeks, I dropped that, too.

I worked full-time at a store, and when I wasn't at work I was lying down watching TV. Sometimes I watched talk shows from 11 A.M. until 5 P.M. I was very lazy, tired all the time. I gained a lot of weight and felt worse and worse about myself.

Then I got even more depressed, quit my job and was stressed most of the day. I was your average couch potato.

During the spring and through the summer, all I remember thinking was "Damn, now I have no job, no money and no school to keep me busy."

This time I was of age to work, but I couldn't find a job.

A New Beginning

But in May I heard about City-As-School, and I decided to apply. It's an alternative high school and you work in the business world for your school credits.

Now that I'm in school, for the most part I enjoy it. Sometimes I get a little hectic and those old feelings come back to haunt me. Like today, I went to school to discuss when I'll be graduating.

I looked at my transcript and I needed so many credits. I thought, "I'm never going to make it."

But you know what, this time I'm going to try to take things at my own steady pace.

I still don't have my act completely together. I'm still struggling. I still have doubts.

When I mess up, it's kind of like a tornado—it swirls and swirls and it doesn't end until it's done with all of its destruction. Then, I pick up the pieces and start over, because the worst has already happened. All that's left is the endless effort to fix and correct.

I Want to Be the Turtle, Not the Hare

Still, I get sad and mad at myself because this is not what I want to be doing with myself.

I guess I'm beginning to think of my life like that old folktale "The Turtle and the Hare." The hare was always looking for the shortcuts, sure he was going to win the race. The turtle took his time.

The hare relaxed. He napped. But soon he awoke and realized the turtle was inches from winning the race. The hare became hectic and tried to rush, but the turtle reached the finish line first, and the hare lost.

I was that silly rabbit—but slowly I'm becoming that turtle. I will make it and reach my finish line. I won't give up.

I'm going to graduate no matter what. I'm going to stay in school and not only prove myself to my family but prove myself to myself.

Chapter 2

Choosing a College

Finding the Right Match for You

Frank C. Leana

For many high school students, the college search process can become stressful as they are deluged with information from many universities and colleges. In the following article, Frank C. Leana argues that the goal of the college search process should be the right match between your abilities and desires and what the college has to offer. He provides advice to students about the college search, including questions students should ask themselves. Leana is an education counselor and author of *The Best Private High Schools*.

For most high school juniors, the college-application process seems like a daunting task. How do you begin to narrow your choices of thousands of colleges to focus on what is right for you? As seniors receive their long-awaited admission envelopes in the spring, juniors first begin to experience those roller-coaster emotions that come with the rite of passage of getting into college.

Chances are that at this time last year, even the now-confident seniors felt as confused as you do about what steps to take to look at college opportunities. But remember that the college-application process is just that: a process. It needs to evolve over time, usually between winter of your junior year and the spring of senior year. Getting into college is as much about what you are looking for in a college as it is about what colleges are looking for in you.

Different colleges have different personalities, just as the students who apply to them. Your job is to get to know those personalities so that you can find your best match. To start, consider the following characteristics.

Going the Distance

How far away from home is it realistically—and financially—possible for you to travel? Airfare is expensive, and it can add a considerable amount to your annual bill. Have you lived away from home before? If you get homesick, will you want to be able to go home for a weekend of home-cooked meals and family? How accessible is public transportation between the colleges you are considering and your home?

Do you prefer the cultural and social stimulation of a city or the pines and mountains of a rural setting? Some colleges (such as Trinity College in Hartford, Connecticut, New York University in Manhattan or the University of Southern California in Los Angeles) are located in cities, where it's just as easy to walk to a movie or order a tuna sandwich at 11 P.M. Other schools (such as Hamilton College in Clinton, New York or Carleton College in Northfield, Minnesota) are some distance from a major city.

Would you like to experience a different region of the country for four years? If so, it is important that you visit there before enrolling. Styles and cultural attitudes (think liberal vs. conservative) differ from region to region. Make sure you are comfortable with the region's prevailing attitudes and values.

Do you prefer a warm to a cold climate? Do you see yourself on a golf course in North Carolina or ski slopes in New Hampshire? Are your moods or your health affected by climate? Do not underestimate the importance of location, environment, and climate on your overall happiness, well-being and success.

Size Matters

Do you learn most effectively in small classes in which students and teachers interact, or do you prefer large lecture halls? At many large universities, freshmen are taught by teaching assistants who are graduate students at that university. Your teaching assistant, not your professor, is often the one who works closest to the students.

Do the subjects that most interest you call for the resources of a large university with a hefty course-offering book? Do you need an observatory, a sophisticated filmmaking resource, a dance studio, a ceramics lab or a department of Chinese studies? Do you seek the broader cultural, racial, or socio-economic diversity usually associated with larger, sometimes more urban settings?

Work Hard

The more selective the institution, the more rigorous and demanding its courses typically are. Check out the median SAT scores of the school's students, the percentage of students who were in the top ten percent of their high school class and the number of graduates who continue in higher education after college.

How hard do you want to work? Do you respond productively to pressure? Be honest about how competitive you are. Some institutions pride themselves on an intellectual atmosphere, such as the University of Chicago and Johns Hopkins in Baltimore. Some schools require you to take courses across several different areas.

Others encourage you to explore different fields by letting you take a course without having to worry about grades. Sarah Lawrence College in Bronxville, New York, uses professors' comments instead of grades. In one-on-one meetings with professors, students must show they've immersed themselves in learning, rather than try to prove they deserve a specific grade.

Special Circumstances

If you have a special focus in mind, choose a college that can satisfy that interest. Some colleges are tied to a religious affiliation, which can mean required service attendance or religion courses. Some institutions, such as the Massachusetts Institute of Technology in Cambridge, Massachusetts, or Rennselaer Polytechnic Institute in Troy, New York, are known for the strength of engineering and computer science courses. Others, such as Hamilton College in Amherst, Massachusetts, are known for their excellence in the arts and humanities. Still others, such as Wharton at the University of Pennsylvania or Babson College in Wellesley, Massachusetts, are known for excellence in business.

> Different colleges have different personalities.

There are art colleges and music conservatories, such as the San Francisco Institute of the Arts or Oberlin Conservatory in Ohio. Some institutions are known for their strong athletic teams. Check what division to which the school belongs to determine if you are qualified for its teams. Some students don't want to play on a sport, but want strong teams to cheer on nonetheless.

Colleges are interested in all of your special talents, from playing the tuba and acting, to singing, debating or cheerleading. Speak to advisors, coaches and department heads about using your talent at school.

Show Me the Money

Colleges can cost anywhere from a few thousand dollars to $30,000 a year. Some give more scholarships and grant money than others. Some are "need-blind," meaning that your need for financial aid isn't a factor in your admission.

Talk frankly with your parents about how much financial help you will need. Some state universities, such as the University of Delaware in Newark and the University of Michigan in Ann Arbor have honors programs for top students that cost less than even some private colleges.

Now that you've thought about what you want in a college and what a college wants from you, you're ready to make the match. Reference rooms of public libraries, guidance offices and bookstores stock a wide variety of college catalogues, indexes and

The 5th Wave   By Rich Tennant

"Here's a good one. 'Located next to an old cemetery, Misery College offers a brooding environment in which students can explore their darker side.'"

Tennant. © by Rich Tennant. Reprinted with permission.

guidebooks. The indexes are filled with data and usually organized alphabetically, by state or by academic disciplines. Some well-known indexes are *Barron's Profiles of American Colleges, Peterson's Guide* and *Princeton Review's Big Book of Colleges.*

Software programs allow you to conduct searches with your college criteria, and will produce a list of colleges to consider. Most colleges also have their own websites, too. One-stop college sites, such as College Board Online, the Princeton Review, and Collegenet, are also available on the Internet.

Be sure to talk with guidance and college counselors, friends in college, your parents and visiting college representatives. Once you have narrowed your initial search to 10 or 12 possibilities, read about them in detailed guidebooks, such as the *Fiske Guide to Colleges*, the *Yale Insider's Guide* or *Princeton Review's Best Colleges.*

These books give a more subjective view than most indexes, as they include opinions of students and faculty. They describe everything from the quality of food and social life to the strongest departments on campus.

Pack the Bags

You are now ready to plan some visits to college campuses. A visit is your most reliable way to get a feel for the campus and to determine if you belong there. Trust your instincts as you walk around, and listen carefully to what tour guides say—as well what they don't. Check out *Visiting College Campuses* by Spenser and Maleson, which is published by the Princeton Review.

Juniors should call ahead to an admissions office to sign up for a campus tour and information session. It may be better to save your personal interview for later, when you have your junior-year grades and test scores in hand. (Keep in mind that most college campuses close down in early May and come to life again in the middle of August.) You can often interview with a local alumnus during your senior year if you can't get back to campus. It is more important to be prepared for the interview than to just get it over with. If you have a friend in college, plan an overnight visit to see what college life is really like, both in and outside of class.

If your finances won't allow you to visit the campus, talk extensively with college counselors and admission representatives. Watch the videos most colleges will send, read view books and guidebooks and try to speak with a current student. Most admission officers are happy to connect you with a student by phone.

Over the past two years, colleges have seen a sizable increase in their applicant pool; many have gone up as much as 12 percent in the last year. This leads to greater selectivity in the admission process. For you, it means it's more critical now than ever to start planning early. Make sure your high school curriculum is challenging, and that you take enough math, science and foreign language classes to meet a college's entrance requirements. Focus on preparing for the PSAT, SAT and ACT, and get involved in a few clubs, sports or volunteer organizations to establish a record of leadership and involvement.

By the fall of your senior year, you may be ready to apply to a college through an early-decision program. This will mean your applications, recommendations, tests and supporting documents have to be mailed as early as November 1. Use the spring of junior year and the summer before senior year to visit campuses and interview with admission representatives.

As you begin your college search, keep in mind that there is more than one "right" college for you. Select two schools that might admit you, two that will probably admit you and one or two that will definitely let you enroll. Understand what colleges are looking for in their applicants, and know what you will bring to the school. Be your own best advocate by planning ahead and presenting yourself well. You will learn about yourself during the college-selection process, about making decisions, and most importantly, about what makes a college right for you.

How Misaligned Ambitions Can Lead to Poor College Choices

Barbara Schneider and David Stevenson

Many American students, argue Barbara Schneider and David Stevenson, aspire to go to college but have unrealistic expectations about how college education will benefit them or their career goals. In the following selection from their book *The Ambitious Generation*, Schneider and Stevenson tell the story of how "Sarah" spent much time, money, and effort going through the prescribed steps for selecting and applying for college. The authors contend, however, that by focusing on the single objective of finding the "right college," Sarah neglected to analyze her career and educational goals and to develop what they call a "life plan" to achieve them. ("Sarah" is a representative composite who the authors created based on interviews with college students.) Schneider and Stevenson believe that many American students make similar misguided decisions, which may explain why many of them eventually drop out of college. Schneider is a professor of sociology at the University of Chicago and senior social scientist at the

Barbara Schneider and David Stevenson, *The Ambitious Generation: America's Teenagers Motivated but Directionless*, New Haven, CT: Yale University Press, 1999. Copyright © 1999 by Yale University. Reproduced by permission.

National Opinion Research Center. Stevenson was a senior policy advisor in the U.S. Department of Education.

Ted and Sue Marshall have three children; their eldest, Sarah, is a junior in college. Sarah was a good student in high school and according to her teachers had shown "some real talent in writing and art design." Sarah's dream was to become the fashion editor for a chic, international publication like *Elle*, her favorite magazine.

For Sarah, however, it was little more than a dream. She had not taken any steps to learn more about the worlds of fashion or publishing. She had not pursued an internship at Arnold's, a local book publishing company, volunteered to do costume design for the high school play, submitted articles for the school newspaper, or enrolled in art classes outside of school.

Sarah did, however, spend a lot of time deciding which college to attend. The decision process had been lengthy and costly. In the fall of her junior year, Sarah took the Princeton Review course to prepare for the college entrance examinations, the SAT and ACT. She carefully followed the high school's guidelines for preparing for college and went to the school's special programs for college admissions, including the college fairs. She met with the school's college counselor, who recommended several colleges based on her interests, listed some teachers to ask for recommendation letters, and handed her a pamphlet on how to fill out college application forms.

Pursuing the "Right" College

Sarah's parents spent little time talking with her about how to pursue a career as a fashion editor, what types of colleges offered appropriate programs, and what courses she should take in college. They did, however, spend considerable resources on helping Sarah select the "right" college. They hired a private college counselor, who recommended seven schools based on Sarah's SAT and ACT scores, her junior-class rank, and her interest in fashion and writing. Two of the colleges on the list were "reach schools," where Sarah was unlikely to be admitted, and two others were "safety schools," places that would be likely to admit her. The remaining three were considered "real possibilities."

In the spring of her junior year, Sarah, her mother, and her father visited seven colleges across the United States. During the trip, she "fell in love" with a college on the East Coast. Ranked one of the best liberal arts colleges in the country, the school had an outstanding reputation in the humanities. Sarah was especially interested in the college because of its close proximity to a major city. Following these campus visits, she made a personal ranking of the schools and began the time-consuming process of applying. Her second choice was not as competitive as the first, but it had a good program in English. She also applied to the remaining five colleges, but her hopes were set on attending her first choice.

The acceptance and rejection letters arrived in the spring of her senior year. Sarah received four of the dreaded thin letters. She had not been admitted to her first, second, or third choices and was wait-listed at her fourth. She was accepted at her two safety schools and at a large state university. Devastated by the rejections, Sarah decided to enroll in one of her safety schools, a small private college in Ohio, where she planned to major in English.

The costs of selecting and attending this college were significant. They included the private counselor ($2,500), college admissions preparation classes ($700), trips to visit colleges ($1,750), and college application fees for the seven schools ($280). The actual bill for attending the college for a year was more than the cost of a moderately priced car; to obtain a bachelor's degree in four years, the total would exceed $100,000. Because of her parents' middle-class income, Sarah was not eligible for financial aid, and she did not receive any scholarship assistance. Her parents were concerned whether she was "making the right choice," given the high costs of the college and her ambivalence about attending one of her safety schools. Their concerns were well founded.

When Sarah enrolled in the school she was unfamiliar with the college curriculum and soon learned that it offered few courses in art or fashion design. In her first semester, she found the English classes very difficult and changed her major to communications. But this decision also proved to be a mistake: the communications courses seemed uninteresting, so she changed her major again, to business. Now a junior, Sarah remains enrolled in the college but still is unsure what she wants to study. She has already changed her major twice and will need an additional semester to earn her bachelor's degree. Sarah feels she has made poor choices. She is not sure this college was the best one for her and worries that she will be unable to find a job after graduating.

Adolescent Ambitions

Sarah's ambitions are similar to those of many American adolescents in the 1990s. Large numbers of them expect to become physicians, lawyers, and business managers; few want to work as machinists, secretaries, or plumbers. Such high ambitions are held by teenagers from all families—rich, poor, Asian, black, Hispanic, and white. More adolescents than ever expect to graduate from college, earn graduate degrees, and work in the white-collar world of professionals. They are America's most ambitious teenage generation ever.

Popular media images often portray adolescents as "slackers," drug users, and perpetrators of violent crimes. The overwhelming majority of teenagers, however, graduate from high school, do not use hard drugs, are not criminals, and do not father or have babies while still in their teens. Many of them are willing to work hard to get good grades and assume this will make them eligible for scholarships at the college they plan to attend. Most young people are worried about their futures and believe attaining a college degree is critical for finding a first real job. The bachelor's degree is seen as the necessary first step in moving up the economic and social ladder. Many consider graduate and professional degrees essential.

Although very ambitious, many adolescents find it very difficult to fulfill their dreams. They are unaware of steps they can take that may help them achieve their ambitions. Often their ambitions are dreamlike and not realistically connected to specific educational and career paths. Regardless of how hard they try, they may find themselves, like Sarah, "running in place and unsure where to go." . . .

Ambitions are an important part of the lives of adolescents. Whether realistic or not, they help teenagers make sense of their lives and their futures. They can use their ambitions like a compass to help chart a life course and to provide direction for spending their time and energy. Ambitions can increase the chances that adolescents will take schoolwork seriously, gain admission to the college of their choice, and view their success as a product of hard work. Ambitions developed during adolescence also have lifelong significance; they influence career choices and future earnings. . . .

Are Today's Adolescents Too Ambitious?

Pursuing a college education is a pervasive desire of today's adolescents. It is fair to ask whether they want more education than is necessary. We find that almost half of these teenagers hope to get degrees that exceed the credentials needed for the occupations they want. . . . Six times more adolescents want to be doctors and five times more want to be lawyers than there are projected to be openings in these professions.

Some high school graduates in the 1990s do not attend college immediately after high school. However, unlike those in the

1950s, today's high school graduates are not likely to obtain well-paying jobs that can lead to long-term, stable employment. The jobs they can get pay poorly and provide few opportunities for career promotion. Facing such job prospects, high school graduates who have entered the workforce hold on to their dreams of attending college and obtaining additional training and skills.

> Most high school students . . . have high ambitions but no clear life plans for reaching them.

Some adolescents have educational and occupational goals that are complementary. We describe these teenagers as having aligned ambitions. Students with aligned ambitions know the type of job they want and how much education is needed to get it. Adolescents with aligned ambitions are more likely to select a path or construct a life plan that enhances their chances of reaching their occupational goals. Life plans are important for transforming ambitions from a dream to an everyday goal. Such plans vary in form, however. We have found that life plans that are coherent with detail and realism are especially useful for choosing a path that increases the probability of success in adulthood. They provide adolescents with a sense of order, encourage them to engage in strategic effort and to sustain high levels of motivation, and help them to use familial and organizational resources.

Most high school students are like Sarah: they have high ambitions but no clear life plans for reaching them. We describe these adolescents as having misaligned ambitions. These "drifting dreamers" have limited knowledge about their chosen occupations, about educational requirements, or about future demand for these occupations. Without such information, their life plans are not realistic and are often ill formed. Drifting dreamers are found among boys and girls and all racial and ethnic groups. . . .

A basic choice today's adolescents face is whether to begin college at a two-year or a four-year institution. More students who expect to obtain a bachelor's or graduate degree are deciding to begin their college studies at two-year institutions. Unfortunately, this decision creates what we describe as an ambition paradox—students with high ambitions choosing an educational route with low odds of success. Students with misaligned ambitions are more likely to be caught in this ambition paradox. . . .

Today's teenagers see their future work lives as filled with promise and uncertainty. They believe in the value of technology, in the importance of being flexible, and in the need for specialization; they also believe that they will change jobs frequently and change careers occasionally. Teenagers accept the volatility of the labor market and believe that the way to create a personal safety net is to obtain additional education. This focus on post-secondary education as a form of security helps to explain the dramatic rise in ambitions. It also makes more apparent the importance of the choices that teenagers make for reaching their dreams. Small choices, such as which courses to take in high school, can influence their preparation for college, and other choices, such as whether to enroll in a two-year or four-year college, can influence their chances of earning a bachelor's degree. Unfortunately, many adolescents make uninformed choices, and the costs of making poor choices can be great. Sarah chose a college that did not offer what she wanted to study; she changed her major several times; and she is about to finish college with little idea of what she wants to do. Sarah and many other adolescents do not have meaningful life plans to help guide them in making choices. Many, like Sarah, believe that college is necessary to obtain a decent job. The time and energy young

> The costs of making poor choices can be great.

people put into going to college and the resources and effort their parents and schools expend in helping them make the transition can be substantial. Many of these efforts, however, focus on a single objective—getting into college—without attention to the formation of ambitions.

The Top Ten Worst Reasons for Selecting a College

Joseph A. Fantozzi Sr.

Joseph A. Fantozzi Sr. is associate director of admissions at Hunter College in New York. In the following article, he responds to a question from a high student seeking advice on making an educated decision about college. Fantozzi answers with a list of reasons students should *not* use when making their choice.

Q: *The college decision process is overwhelming me. It's stressful and confusing . . . I don't know how much more I can take. Any advice on how I can chill out, and make an educated decision?*

A: The average college-bound high school junior or senior spends a great deal of time researching colleges (you're reading this, aren't you?). With all the college fairs, tours, open houses, Web searches, and pre-admission interviews, it's no wonder you're confused.

And guess what?! Despite all the information available, many students select a college for all the wrong reasons, some of which are enough to send a guidance counselor into retirement (or back to the classroom!). Based on actual conversations with members of the class of 2000, here are this year's "Top Ten Worst Reasons" for selecting a college. . .

Money Concerns

10. *It's the cheapest.* Don't assume that you can't afford an expensive college, even if your family doesn't qualify for government aid. Most private colleges offer scholarships of their own, including many that are merit-based. Even if you are not a top student (although that certainly helps!), you may possess some other quality for which an alumnus or private donor has set up a special scholarship. Contact the admissions or financial aid office at the college for more information.

9. *It's the most expensive.* On the other hand, don't assume that the higher the tuition, the better the school. Public colleges are often able to provide a high quality education at a reasonable price thanks to government support. Also, if you plan to continue your education beyond the degree, spending less on your undergraduate education means having more funds available for graduate or professional school.

8. *They've offered me the most scholarship money.* Don't compare apples with oranges. If college "A" is offering $5,000 in grants, and college "B" is only offering $1,000, college "A" must be the better deal, right? Not necessarily! Subtract the amount of grants from the total cost of education at each school in order to get the real cost of attending. And remember: Most scholarships have conditions attached (i.e., you must maintain full-time status and a certain grade point average in order to retain the award).

7. *"I know I'll get in."* While it's important to apply to a "safety school," one for which you are well qualified, don't cross your dream college off the list without first doing your homework. Although most schools are vague when it comes to revealing admissions criteria, you can get a sense

of your chances of acceptance by reviewing the profile of the previous year's freshman class. Ask about the mean SAT score, the range of high school averages, the number of students with a class ranking similar to yours, and the percentage of all applicants that were accepted. If you think you might be a "borderline" case, find out which secondary factors are considered (e.g., interviews, essays, letters of recommendation, extra curricular activities, etc.) and make sure you are competitive in these areas.

6. *They offer the hottest "Who-Wants-To-Be-a-Millionaire-By-Age-25" major.* While it's fine to set high goals for yourself (including financial goals), it's important to be realistic. No college can guarantee financial success for each of its graduates. That's not to say you won't be a millionaire by age 25, but it's going to depend largely on your ambition, hard work, and luck. Also, since many college students end up changing majors, it's a good idea to enroll at a college that has a wide selection of programs.

Be Careful About Rankings

5. *They're ranked number one in the "Moron's Guide to Colleges and Universities."* There are a number of excellent guidebooks that offer information about colleges and universities, all of which should be considered important resources in your selection process. However, be careful about those rankings. Take a good look at the criteria on which the rankings are based; some of these factors may not be all that important to you. Stick to the hard facts (student-faculty ratio, class size, percentage of courses taught by teaching assistants, etc.).

4. *The campus is pretty.* Although aesthetics are important (after all, you don't want to spend the next four years in a dump), you need to look beyond the beautiful to the practical. Most college campuses look great on a crisp

fall day, which is why open houses tend to be held then. Remember that come February, you may be crossing that quad with a stiff winter breeze blowing at the icicles forming on your nose. If it's a very large campus, ask about transportation between buildings.

3. *My favorite celebrity went there.* Colleges love to turn to successful, well-known alumni when promoting their schools. This is fine, as long as the alum's degree is fairly recent and had something to do with their accomplishments. If a highly successful Wall Street executive majored in business six years ago at Lotsabucks U., that might be an indication of the quality of that school's business program. However, if a philosophy major from the College of Existentialism happens to become a famous actress 20 years after graduating, that doesn't really tell you much about the college's quality.

2. *It's a great party school.* It's important to pick a school that has an active campus life, whether you plan to live on campus or commute. A major part of your college experience, after all, will come from interacting with other students in clubs, organizations, and social situations. If there are too many distractions, however, you may have difficulty concentrating on studying, not to mention attending 8 A.M. classes.

And, finally (drum roll, please!) . . . The NUMBER ONE WORST REASON TO SELECT A COLLEGE:

1. *"It's where my boyfriend or girlfriend is going."* Get real! If the relationship ends, you may find yourself scratching your head, trying to figure out how you ended up at a college that doesn't suit you in any way. If the relationship survives, the distraction might just affect your grades and/or stifle your social life. Either way, you'll most likely find yourself wishing you'd given your college choice more serious thought.

Looking Beyond the Most Selective Schools

Edward Tenner

Many high school students have their hearts set on attending one of America's elite and most selective schools. In the following article, Edward Tenner urges them to consider other options. He argues that many colleges and universities can provide just as strong an education as elite institutions such as Harvard University. Indeed, a person's future success depends more on one's own efforts and initiative than on what school they go to. Tenner is a historian and author of *Why Things Bite Back: Technology and the Revenge of Unintended Consequences.*

A re the numbers getting you down, the 10- or 12-to-1 odds against admission to the most selective colleges? Things could be worse. You could be a Ph.D. looking for a job. For more than 25 years, competition for most faculty positions has made acceptance to the Ivy League look easy. A single position in physics drew up to 1,000 applications in the early 1990s, according to Edwin Goldin, director of career services at the American Institute of Physics. A recent Ph.D. in American literature reports receiving rejection letters from departments with 500 to

700 applicants; it took him several years to find a community-college job.

A Bright Side

The challenges faced by job-seeking faculty have a bright side for college applicants. For years, schools deep in the first tier and below it have been able to hire candidates who in the 1950s and 1960s would have gone to work at a top-ranked school. Many are attracting first-rate students too. Down the road from Princeton at Rider University, which was founded as a business college, I've met people like Linda Materna, a wonderful specialist in Spanish drama (who has taught at Princeton too), and James Dickinson, a pathbreaking sociologist whose interests range from economic development to the arts and urbanism. The California State system boasts renowned scholars like the classicist and military historian Victor Davis Hanson at Fresno and my graduate-school friend, the music historian William Weber, at Long Beach.

At the same time, even the most selective schools have decided they can't afford to be uniformly strong. Princeton's department of geosciences opted in the 1980s to discontinue vertebrate paleontology, donated most of its fossils to Yale and focused instead on other earth sciences. Massachusetts Institute of Technology (MIT) has a writing program; Caltech doesn't. The University of Utah's computer-science department doesn't have the robotics of Carnegie Mellon but is famous for graphics. While the U.S. News ratings are an excellent measure of many qualities that matter in education, a school's overall rank should be far less important in your analysis of where to go than the details of what a school offers to you.

One result of specialization and the trickle down of talent is that hyperselective schools are not the only ones with world-class programs. Geography is a school, not just a department, at Clark University in Worcester, Massachusetts; Harvard abolished its geography department decades ago. Rutgers has a whole school of communication and information studies; Princeton has no department in either field. Rensselaer Polytechnic is a leader in lighting studies, Virginia Tech in human-machine interaction; you won't find comparable programs at Caltech. Yes, the Top 20 offer more good elective courses and generally have better libraries and laboratories. But thanks to the Internet, even small rural schools can offer formidable numbers of online journals.

A True Gap?

Graduates of highly selective colleges do make more money. But they seem to be successful partly because their families are more affluent and better connected than the average, and partly because they have strengths that would have gone with them to any college. A recent study by Stacy Dale of the Andrew W. Mellon Foundation and Alan B. Krueger of Princeton revealed that among 1976 high school graduates accepted at both highly selective and moderately selective colleges, those attending the latter were actually earning slightly more than those who chose the top schools: an average of $91,200 in 1995 versus $90,100. (Students from lower-income families did significantly better after attending elite colleges.)

What do these trends mean for a student researching colleges today? Plan to explore your options widely. You're probably going to change careers several times, so you'll want to consider taking subjects you didn't in high school. A strong general education will support you as you advance in your original field, or change. Are the available student activities ones that matter to you? Ask where recent graduates have continued their education. Franklin and Marshall, which accepts more than half its applicants, is known for strong science teaching and excellent medical-school placement. Above all, don't listen to anxiety-mongers. Selective schools aren't and never were the gatekeepers of opportunity. You're the one who holds the keys.

Choosing a Women's College

BriAnne Dopart

While most colleges and universities in the United States are coeducational, there remain some single-sex institutions in which only women or men attend. BriAnne Dopart is a student at Smith College, a women's college in Massachusetts. In this selection she writes of her decision to attend that institution, her initial doubts about going to a single-sex school, and what she gains by being part of a legacy of women helping women.

When the acceptance letter came, my mother cried. It was the last letter to come of the five colleges I had applied to and it was the only all girls school I'd thought of. Applying to Smith was more my mother's idea than mine. I agreed to try because I never thought they would take me. I was wrong.

The first brochure I'd ever seen for a women's college had a picture of several well-dressed white women sitting on plush chairs and sipping tea from delicate china. The women looked involved in some serious discussion. Underneath the photo was a caption explaining that at this particular women's college, tea was held every Friday afternoon providing women with the chance to relax and wind down after a hard week at school.

I remember laughing at the picture and telling my mother that she must be dreaming. I liked spending time with women, but that didn't mean I wanted to be surrounded by only women. I called myself a feminist, but that didn't mean I was a feminist and nothing else. I didn't want to go to a place where my gender was a focal [central] point. I had other things to think about; I had other things to say.

> Going to a women's college wasn't what I had imagined in high school.

When I first thought of college, I thought of freedom. I pictured a community that was made up of only young, intelligent, active, and open-minded 20-somethings. I imagined parties, political rallies, all-night conversations, delivery pizza, and 20-ounce slurpees. Tea was not in my fantasy. Neither were knee-high stockings.

The reasons I actually went to a single-sex college bear more heavily on twists of fate and coincidence than they do a well thought out decision. Going to a women's college wasn't what I had imagined in high school. Going to college at all wasn't necessarily what I had imagined in high school. However, the fall after I graduated from a tiny high school in central New Jersey, I was waving good bye to my parents from the steps of my new home in New England—a women's college in a small Western Massachusetts town that housed 2,500 other women.

I had told my parents I would try Smith. I had no desire to stay there, and I certainly wasn't going to try to like it. Weeks after being here, though, I realized that I wasn't alone. Everyone I met had thought of other schools. Everyone had reservations about going to a women's college. Everyone was scared to death of being not smart enough, not independent enough, and of not making friends.

Despite my doubts, I couldn't help but feel some strain of pride for my college. Walking around campus, I couldn't help but feel like I was a part of something so much bigger than the differences between tea and slurpees—I was part of a place that defined itself by its ability and goal to educate women. I went to a school that existed for the advancement and encouragement of women in particular.

Even now that I'm happy here and I have wonderful friends, wonderful teachers, and a clear idea of why I'm here, I still have moments where I wish I was any place else. But so do my friends at other colleges.

After two and a half years in a women's school, I know that I belong to a legacy far older than that of any college: the legacy of women supporting, teaching, loving, befriending, and sustaining other women. Every day I go to school, I know that legacy is alive.

Money Concerns and Financial Aid

Anne Austin

Money is a major concern for many high school students (and their parents) who are weighing college options. Tuition and living expenses at many four-year colleges can top one hundred thousand dollars. In the following article, writer Anne Austin argues that college should be viewed as an investment in the future. She explains that government and private financial aid programs can help most students attend the college of their choice. In addition, Austin describes how financial aid is calculated, explains the differences between scholarships, grants, and loans, and offers suggestions for cutting costs.

Think of college as an investment in your future. Studies show that college graduates earn 77 percent more than those with only a high school diploma. If you look at the potential earnings, you really can't afford *not* to go.

College can be a hefty investment, though. *Peterson's Guide to College* estimates that four years at a private college can cost up to $100,000; the same degree from a state school could run $30,000 to $50,000. But don't let sticker shock scare you away. Approximately $68 billion in aid was available, according to a study released by the College Board [in 2001]. The federal government distributed $30 billion to 7 million students; colleges distributed another $8 billion. The remaining aid came from a variety of sources.

How Financial Aid Is Figured

To find out about a financial aid package, start with the school's "cost of attendance." This is the amount it costs a student to pay for the whole experience—tuition, fees, books, room and board, transportation, and personal expenses.

Subtract from that amount the "Expected Family Contribution (EFC)," calculated from the financial information your parents submit concerning both income and expenses of the family. EFC should be funded out of cash, savings, and loans, and not from current earnings alone.

Don't panic if the difference looks like more money than you can afford. It's the amount that needs to be financed with aid. Financial aid specialists recommend you apply for aid whether or not you think you'll qualify. Submit the FAFSA (Free Application for Federal Student Aid) and any forms the school requires. Above all, meet the deadlines.

The financial aid office will put together a package with a combination of the four basic forms of aid: scholarships, grants, loans, and work-study.

> Don't let sticker shock scare you away.

1. Scholarships. Scholarships are the best form of aid because the money does not have to be repaid. The application process often requires you to write a special essay or be interviewed. Scholarships are generally awarded for merit.

Scholarship sources can include the college itself, civic clubs, unions, foundations, and religious groups. Most states offer scholarship programs to residents to attend in-state colleges. Usually, these are awarded based on grades and financial need.

To find out what's available, a good place to start is the scholarship database at *www.finaid.com* and similar sites. . . . Beware of services that ask you to pay a fee to locate money—they usually are scams.

2. Grants. Grants are also awards of money that do not have to be repaid. Unlike scholarships, the primary eligibility requirement for a grant is financial need. Need is calculated using a formula established by the federal or state government. The largest grant program is the Pell Grant, funded by the federal government. Students received up to $3,300 in the 2000–2001 academic year, the amount increases slightly from year to year.

> As with any big investment, take time to plan and explore your options.

3. Loans. Loans are financial aid that you have to repay. Fifty-nine percent of all aid is in the form of loans; the average student graduates with a loan/debt of $16,500.

The best source is the Federal Stafford Loan program. You won't begin making payments until you leave school. Students with exceptional financial need may qualify for the federally funded, campus-based Perkins Loan.

Your parents may qualify for a PLUS (Parent Loan for Undergraduate Students) as a way to cover the EFC (Expected Family Contribution). Home equity loans or a line of credit are also possibilities.

4. Work-Study. The fourth form of aid is work-study. The work-study program on most campuses is a two-part program. In order to qualify for federal work-study, the student must meet federal eligibility based on financial need. The college provides the job, but the federal government pays part of the wage (the student doesn't see a split check, but this makes a big difference to the institution's ability to hire students). The college also might offer institutional work-study, which has no eligibility requirements other than the student be qualified to do the job.

Usually students are allowed to work 20 hours a week. Pay is minimum wage unless the job they fill is more specialized. Students often work as lab assistants in computer labs, shelvers in the library, and clerks. They may also do data entry and filing in college offices, and so on. The main advantages are that the work is on campus, the employer works around the student's schedule, and the student has the ability to make contacts or get experience if the work is in the area of his or her major.

Average and Range of Tuition and Fee Charges at Postsecondary Institutions, 2001–2002

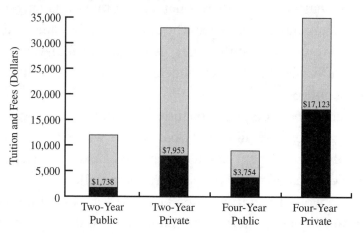

Annual Survey of Colleges, The College Board, New York, NY, 2001.

If you're willing to commit several years after graduation to work for the government or another agency, you can work a deal. Government agencies at both the state and federal levels offer "loan forgiveness" or scholarship programs. A scholarship program pays your costs upfront. In a loan forgiveness program, you pay for college upfront with loans, etc., and the agency pays off the loans for you. Federal programs include the National Service Scholarship Program, AmeriCorps, Learn and Serve America, and Senior Corps. States often offer loan forgiveness to students in under-represented fields such as teaching and health care.

The military will fund college with a similar arrangement. Last year [2001], more than 50,000 students enrolled in campus ROTC [Reserve Officers Training Corps] programs; 17,500 of those have scholarships. Veterans and their dependents also may qualify for special aid money.

Cutting Costs

In addition to applying for aid, think about ways to reduce costs. Forty-four percent of students begin at lower-priced community colleges. After evaluating all her aid offers, Tracy Turner decided to go this route. "Both my parents are in college and own their own businesses, so there's not a lot of money. I can get my prerequisites and then transfer. The courses are the same, but the cost . . . wow, what a difference!" A number of four-year institutions offer scholarships to students who transfer from community colleges.

In high school, look into concurrent enrollment at a local college to get some requirements out of the way early. Take as many advanced placement classes as you can. That way, you'll have fewer classes you'll need to pay for in college.

Plan to work. Even if you aren't eligible for work-study, consider working either during the school year or during the summers. Think about co-op experiences during college so you can get paid for work experience related to your field.

As with any big investment, take time to plan and explore your options. Then watch that investment pay off!

Point of Contention: Should Most Students Be Advised to Go to College?

Prior to World War II, less than 5 percent of the American population held a college degree. A college education was seen as something appropriate for the academic (and social) elite, not a necessity for most Americans. Following World War II, the G.I. Bill, by paying for the college educations of returning U.S. veterans, ushered in a new era of mass higher education. It not only made college education more affordable for many middle- and working-class Americans, but it also raised educational expectations for succeeding generations. Today, surveys indicate that nine out of ten high school seniors expect to go to college. Advocates of college education tout it not only as a way to become a well-educated person, but as an essential tool to succeed in today's job market.

However, not everyone agrees that the rising popularity of college is a positive social trend. Some critics believe that many high school seniors who express an intention to attend college may not truly benefit from a college education and are being hurt by bad advice. Many students who go to college find themselves struggling in remedial classes and eventually drop out. The large and increasing costs of a college education, which can leave many students in serious debt, is another point of concern of those who believe that some college students may be better off in vocational schools or in the workplace.

What should high school students be advised about college? The following articles provide different answers to that question. Katharine Hansen, a former college instructor and editor of *Quintzine*, an electronic newsletter for jobseekers, contends that a college education is a necessity for all students. Conversely, Richard Rothstein, an education reporter for the *New York Times*, argues that college is not the best option for many students.

A College Education Is a Necessity in Today's World

Katharine Hansen

Questioning whether you should go to college? Here are five ways that a college education will make you a better person:

1. It will likely make you more prosperous.
2. It will give you a better quality of life.
3. It will give you the power to change the world.
4. It will be something you can pass on to your children.
5. It makes you a major contributor to the greatest nation on earth.

Money

First things first, because I know you're thinking "Show me the money." The lifetime income of families headed by individuals with a bachelor's degree will be about $1.6 million *more* than the incomes of families headed by those with a high-school diploma, according to the Postsecondary Education Opportunity Research Letter. The U.S. Census Bureau tells us that in 1999, average income for a male age 25 or over who holds a bachelor's degree was about $61,000, compared to about $32,000 for a male with a high-school diploma—so the college graduate's income was about $29,000 more annually than the high-school grad's. And incomes of those with only a high-school education are sinking steadily lower.

Now, unfortunately, women still make less money than men do, but the news for females who choose higher education is truly phenomenal: In a 1997 study, young women who had completed a bachelor's degree or higher earned *91 percent* more than young women with no more than a high-school diploma or GED (General Education Development certificate).

A college education is an extraordinarily profitable investment. Every dollar spent on a young man's college education produces $34.85 in increased lifetime income. Any Wall Street stockbroker would envy that kind of investment yield—especially these days. You say you can't afford to go to college? The Postsecondary Education Opportunity Research Letter says you can't afford not to.

College may be expensive, but the only thing more expensive than getting a college education is *not* getting one. The income differential empowers you to make choices that enrich your life.

> A college education is an extraordinarily profitable investment.

Unlike most purchases, a college education appreciates in value instead of depreciating. And don't forget that there are ways to get around the high cost—scholarships, financial aid, community colleges, and emerging choices in distance learning that can enable you to take classes on your computer while also participating in the workforce. . . .

John G. Ramsay, a professor at the Perlman Center for

Learning and Teaching, said that the credentials you gain with a college education "are about setting yourself apart, being employable, becoming a legitimate candidate for a job with a future. They are about climbing out of the dead-end job market, and achieving one of life's most difficult developmental tasks: independence from one's parents. Strong credentials trigger that magical set of middle class 'firsts,'" Ramsay said: "The first real-world job, the first non-student apartment, the first new car, and of course, the first loan payments. Weak credentials can be painful reminders of a string of misfortunes: poor advice, money problems, bad decisions, and wasted time."

> A college education is a legacy for your children.

Quality of Life

Next, quality of life. Is there anyone who wouldn't like to live a longer, healthier life? Studies show that, compared to high-school graduates, college graduates have:

- longer life spans
- better access to health care
- better dietary and health practices
- greater economic stability and security
- more prestigious employment and greater job satisfaction
- less dependency on government assistance
- greater use of seat belts
- more continuing education
- greater Internet access
- greater attendance at live performances
- greater participation in leisure and artistic activities
- more book purchases
- higher voting rates

- greater knowledge of government
- greater community service and leadership
- more volunteer work
- more self-confidence
- and less criminal activity and incarceration.

Social Change

Thirdly, more money and greater quality of life aren't the only reasons for a college education. Children's Defense Fund director Marian Wright Edelman cautioned that "Once you have that college diploma in hand never work just for money or power. They won't save your soul or build a decent family or help you sleep at night."

Edelman explains why this advice is so important: "We are the richest nation on earth, yet our incarceration, drug addiction, and child poverty rates are among the highest in the industrialized world. Don't condone or tolerate moral corruption, whether it's found in high or low places, whatever its color. . . . Don't confuse legality with morality. Dr. [Martin Luther] King Jr. noted that everything Adolf Hitler did was legal. Don't give anyone the proxy for your conscience."

Cuban patriot Jose Marti once wrote: "Students are the ramparts and the strongest army of freedom. When liberty is in danger, a newspaper threatened, a ballot box in peril, the students unite. . . . And arm in arm they go through the streets demanding justice, or they run printing presses in cellars for what they cannot say."

If you doubt that knowledge is power, consider the societies that have denied education to selected segments of the population. The Taliban in Afghanistan keeps women from having any power by outlawing their education, much as antebellum American society kept slaves from possessing

lenying them schooling [the United States routed
in its war against terrorism in 2001].

ns of higher learning continue to be among the
for cultivating social change.

A Legacy for Your Children

The fourth point is that a college education is a legacy for your children. The idea of having children may be as remote to you as the international space station, but trust us, your college education will benefit your children—and not just so you can impress them with how well you play *Who Wants to Be a Millionaire?*

Research shows that children of college-educated parents are healthier, perform better academically, and are more likely to attend college themselves than children of those with lower educational attainment.

Your education builds a foundation for your children—for our nation's children, and for the children of our global community—which leads to the last point.

College and the American Dream

Education is the cornerstone of public progress.

Education is the essence of the democratic ideals that elevated the United States from a backward land of rebellious colonists to the greatest, most spirited, powerful and successful nation in the world.

And we are the greatest nation. America leads the world in educational attainment, and with only one exception, we lead in per-capita income. Speaking at a symposium on American values, Anne L. Heald said there is "an extraordinary consensus that the preparation of young people for work is one of the singular most important things a society can do to improve its ability to prosper in a new international economy."

Similarly, Federal Reserve Board Chairman Alan Greenspan said recently, "We must ensure that our whole population receives an education that will allow full and continuing participation in this dynamic period of American economic history."

What Greenspan is saying is that, without college, you may be left out. And the relationship between a college education and success will become more and more significant in our information-driven global economy. Higher education will be increasingly important for landing high-paying jobs.

Technology and the information age are not the only reasons to be well educated; the trend is toward multiple jobs and even multiple careers, and higher education prepares you to make the transitions to new fields.

So what more could you ask of your investment in higher education than prosperity, quality of life, the knowledge that bolsters social change, a legacy for your children, and the means to ensure the continuing success of the American dream?

Katharine Hansen, "What Good Is a College Education Anyway?" *Quintzine*, vol. 2, November 5, 2001. Copyright © 2001 by *Quintzine*. Reproduced by permission.

College Is Not the Best Option for Many Students

Richard Rothstein

Heidi Leonard is a career and college counselor in Newport Beach, Calif., where most parents are college-educated professionals. Recently, Ms. Leonard advised a high school student with poor grades but a passion for automobiles, finding him an internship at an elite racing car company.

She thought it could lead to a well-paid career. But the boy's parents were incensed, insisting that he go to college. Ms. Leonard suspects he will soon drop out and take less desirable work than the internship he rejected.

The College Illusion

This kind of thing is happening all over the country because of an illusion that college is for everyone and that a high-tech future requires as many college graduates as possible. Yet the Department of Labor expects only about a fourth of future jobs to require college degrees.

Barbara Schneider and David Stevenson, authors of *The Ambitious Generation: America's Teenagers, Motivated but Directionless* (1999), say exaggerated beliefs about job needs can have dire results. Some 90 percent of seniors say they will go to college. Some 35 percent want to be engineers, architects, health professionals, social or natural scientists. But only 8 percent of openings will be in those fields.

> Two-thirds of [high school] graduates enroll in college, but only half of these get bachelor's degrees by their late 20s.

Many youths face this reality only after high school. Two-thirds of graduates enroll in college, but only half of these get bachelor's degrees by their late 20s. Another 15 percent finish community college. More than a third drop out with no degree, though some may return later.

It is often said that without college a youth will be "flipping hamburgers." But many good jobs—computer and health technicians, equipment repair or finance personnel—demand vocational or on-the-job training, not bachelor's degrees.

Students who are unsuited for college but still attend may lose the chance for such jobs. In their cases, the flipping hamburgers myth could become reality.

Parental Objections

If all races and social classes have similar academic ability, then even in middle-class suburbs a goodly number of students should incline to technical careers. But parents won't hear of it.

In some suburbs—Montclair, N.J., is one—counselors are pressured to get almost all students into college because if admission rates fall, children may switch to private schools. So youngsters are guided to universities even when they would benefit more from technical training.

In less affluent communities too, uncritical college ambitions can impede counseling. Indeed, black adolescents plan on college at higher rates than whites. Glenda Rose, a high school adviser in Miami, says her efforts to help minority students get into technical schools are resisted by parents who believe a university education is now essential. Many students then drop out of college to take less rewarding jobs than those for which training programs prepare.

Ms. Rose blames the media, church leaders and former President Bill Clinton (who urged universal college) for parents' misconceptions.

Of course, job readiness is not the only reason for college, perhaps not the best reason. But today's push to prepare all students to attend does not mostly come from concern for their moral, cultural or intellectual growth. It stems from vocational myths.

Confusing Ability with Race and Class

This will be tough to fix because aiming too low is worse than aiming too high. Counselors who urge some students to pursue nonacademic paths may confuse ability with race and class. The affluent have traditionally gone to college while minority and working-class children were tracked to training programs or workplaces, even when their talent justified college ambitions.

But asking everyone to attend college does not serve all students well. Nor should universities have to devote resources to failing youngsters who don't belong.

Somehow we've got to guide fewer students to college while also ensuring that higher education is more accessible to the disadvantaged.

A first step should be adding counselors with improved training. Nationwide, there is now only one counselor for every 560 pupils, handling not only college and career advice but scheduling and discipline. Students cannot get good guidance with so little attention.

Schools also need more business partners to set up internships and other school-to-work programs. Adolescents can then experience an adult world of more than doctors and lawyers on the one hand and fast-food workers on the other. But better counseling cannot thrive in a climate of unreality. No pupils should be impeded by race or class from striving for prestigious professions.

> Asking everyone to attend college does not serve all students well.

This, however, should not mean telling all that they can make it.

Richard Rothstein, "One Answer on College Doesn't Fit All Graduates," *New York Times*, August 15, 2001. Copyright © 2001 by The New York Times Company. Reproduced by permission.

Chapter 3

The Admissions Game

Advice from High School Seniors on Applying to College

Ashley Rudolph and Philip Rucker

Ashley Rudolph and Philip Rucker were high school seniors (class of 2002) who had gone through the college application process when they wrote the following essay. They draw on their own experiences to give advice on the steps students need to take in applying to colleges. Among the important points to remember, they argue, is to be aware of deadlines and to be involved in school and community activities.

Four years ago we both sat in class thinking, 'What am I getting myself into?' At times, those years felt like decades. Other times they felt like weeks. They were filled with both successes and failures—thankfully, the successes outweighed the failures. After devoting the past four years to college admissions, we await the verdict and reflect on the lessons we've learned during the process.

Hopefully you can pick up a few pointers along the way. Take out your pen and paper, you're in for a ride.

The Application Process

After applying to colleges, admissions officers reviewed our applications. These are people who work for the admissions department at a college and are in charge of reading and calculating applications. At some larger universities acceptance may depend on a calculated score based on your grade point average, SAT score, class rank, and high school course load.

The college application process is personal. Admissions counselors know our grades, our SAT scores, where our parents graduated from, and even what our teachers think of us—something we wish we knew.

The process is also competitive. For example, at Yale University in Connecticut, some 15,000 students applied for 1,300 spots in the freshman class this year [2002].

Prepare Early

When you enter high school in the ninth grade, be sure to meet with your guidance counselor and your parents to create a planned curriculum. Decide which courses to take and when. Select courses to prepare you for Advanced Placement (AP) courses in later years.

"The courses that you chose to take throughout high school are crucial since they indicate your level of motivation, initiative, academic risk-taking, intellectual curiosity, and sense of purpose," said Judy R. Wilburn, director of college counseling at St. Andrew's School on Wilmington Island.

Don't fret if your school does not offer many AP classes. Colleges will take into consideration the courses offered at your school when evaluating your course load.

Stand Out

Usually, teen-agers don't want to stand out in the crowd. But trust us, find something that makes you stand out. Whether it's a sport, hobby, or special talent, make it known. For example,

Philip was an accomplished figure skater from California. He lived away from home to train for competitive figure skating since the age of 10. What do you think Philip wrote about in his college essay? You guessed it, his love for ice skating. Meanwhile, Ashley has been an active Girl Scout since she was 5 years old. Therefore, talking about the valuable things she has gained and her stature in the Girl Scouting community made a perfect essay topic.

> At Yale University . . . , some 15,000 students applied for 1,300 spots.

"Real involvement and commitment to outside activities should provide material for essays that will come across as sincere and showing what you are really like as an individual. Part-time job experience can also serve this purpose," Wilburn said.

Speaking of essays, a well-written, unusual and personal essay can turn heads. Keep your essay personal and focused, use humor and write from the heart. Ashley spent countless hours sitting at the computer trying to figure out what the admissions committee would want to hear. It wasn't until a five-minute chat session with her parents in their kitchen that she realized she knew exactly what to write. Sometimes added pressure doesn't help. Take some paper and a pen to your favorite spot and start jotting down anything that comes to your head. The admissions committee wants you to write about what interests you, not what you believe they want to hear.

Getting Involved

Be sure to get involved. Join clubs at school and develop leadership positions in those clubs. Also get involved in the community. Often, in the newspaper, area agencies will post ads or articles asking for help. For example, this fall many local teens volunteered at the Habitat for Humanity Build-a-thon because they heard about it through the paper. Make sure to find something that you enjoy doing, so you will be more likely to continue. Ask your guidance counselors about possible organizations outside of school—the United Way, Youth Commission, hospital volunteer, church leader, or even SAVVY.

Be Organized and on Time

Be sure to get all your forms in on time. When you are applying to nearly a dozen colleges, it can be difficult to remember all those dates. Remember, many schools are unlikely to accept you if you mistake a Dec. 31 deadline for Jan. 31.

"Our selection committee simply couldn't agree on which one of you should get the last opening at the college. So, if you'll just hold the spoons there for as long as you can . . . Martin—are you timing this?"

Tennant. © by Rich Tennant. Reprinted with permission.

Be organized. You must keep in mind that your guidance counselor sends applications for all the seniors at your school—not just you. Be sure to give him/her ample time to write their recommendation. Your recommendation letter will not be very positive if you ask your counselor to write it overnight. For example, make a different folder for each college application. Keep any letters, catalogs, application forms you receive from that college in one folder and keep all your folders in a central location.

Looking back to the month of December [2001], Ashley closes her eyes to keep the bad thoughts from invading her head. On top of having final exams and preparing for winter break, Ashley was rampantly filling out applications after learning of her deferral from Princeton. Though her counselor had advised her to go ahead and complete some applications before her decision day on Dec. 15, she had decided against it. Lesson learned: Listen to those with experience and remember, when you put things off, they only come back to haunt you in the end.

> Find something that makes you stand out.

During this hectic time Ashley was happy to discover the Common Application. The Common Application, which can be found at www.commonapp.org, is a single application that is accepted at more than 200 schools nationwide. Luckily for Ashley, 4 of the 5 schools she applied to accepted this form of application. There is only one catch when using the Common Application—the applicant must be sure to check for any supplemental information required by the school. For example, Yale required two additional essays while Dartmouth required a peer recommendation and additional personal information.

Winter Downtime—Yeah Right!

The majority of colleges and universities will not inform applicants of their admission decision until early April. Therefore you will have three months of waiting to work on scholarships and grades. For some students, Mid-Year Reports are also a big part of the application process and can make that needed difference. A Mid-Year Report is a form the applicant's college counselor fills out informing the school of the applicant's current grades and any new information or awards. Many schools require a Mid-Year Report to complete a student's application. This can be your last time to shine so remember, grades still matter even though you have submitted your application.

> Be sure to get all your forms in on time.

Any new information is welcome at an admissions office. However, be sure that the supplementary information is different than the original information you previously filed. Check with your guidance counselor before sending any supplementary information to the admissions office.

During the winter months be sure to maintain your needed connections with any schools to which you applied. Some schools such as the University of Georgia and Georgia Tech have Web sites where you can check your application status. If you are an athlete who hopes to pursue sports at the collegiate level be sure to send out a letter and sports resume to any coaches at each of your prospective schools. This will allow them to become familiar with your name and watch for your application.

Where's the Money?

Tuitions at most private colleges have skyrocketed above $30,000 per year. Unless you are the rare millionaire and your parents can afford to spend $35,000 per year for you to attend college, join the "financial aid club." Most students attend college by earning a scholarship, taking out a loan, working a part-time job on campus, or a combination of the three. In fact, many selective colleges claim to meet "100 percent of the family's demonstrated financial need." This means that if the college costs $35,000 and the family can only pay $15,000 per year, the college will help you fund the remaining $20,000 by a scholarship grant, loan, or campus job.

Just when you think you're done filling out forms, you've only just begun. Financial aid forms are long and involved but can be easy. First, familiarize yourself with the different forms. There's the FAFSA, which is a Federal Aid Form for all colleges. Then, there's the CSS Profile, another financial aid form sponsored by The College Board, which only some schools require.

Make sure your parents file their taxes on time, if not early, because having their present W2 and tax return forms on hand will make applying for financial aid much easier.

Another way to earn scholarships is from corporations and community organizations that sponsor scholarship competitions, both at the local and national level. Compete for every scholarship you can. By the end, your chances for getting a scholarship are much greater. Our best scholarship advice is to allocate one day when you can work on your scholarships and get them done right then. The worst thing to do is to procrastinate—you want to take your time and do your best on these applications.

Lastly, have fun and don't burn out. After all, you'll want to enjoy college when you finally get there.

College Admissions Experts Discuss What Makes a Winning Application

Devon Powers

The first step high school students take after selecting one or more colleges to apply to is filling out college applications. In the following article by Devon Powers, first published in *Teen People* magazine, a college application by a *Teen People* intern is dissected by two admissions experts: Ted O'Neill of the University of Chicago and Thomas H. Parker of Amherst College in Massachusetts. The two provide suggestions on how students can make their applications stand out. Among their points is to take questions on the applications seriously and to be honest in your responses. Powers is an editorial assistant with *Teen People* magazine.

Y ou spend months taking tests, getting recommendations and fitting long answers to profound questions into tiny spaces. Then comes the fun part: You send in your application and let total strangers decide your fate. We asked two of these all-powerful people—Ted O'Neill, dean of admissions at the University of Chicago, and Thomas H. Parker, dean of admissions and financial aid at Amherst College—to dispel the mystery by explaining the selection process. A brave News Team member even volunteered to let us put one of her applications under the microscope (but asked to remain anonymous). Here are some of the lessons we learned.

> Expressing interest in a major won't affect your chances at most schools.

Decide whether you're going to type or handwrite your application, and then stick to the format. "She jumps back and forth," notes Parker, referring to our applicant's handiwork. "It seems sloppy." And take it seriously when you're instructed to use the space allotted—it makes the pages easier for the admissions pros to read.

Don't worry: Expressing interest in a major won't affect your chances at most schools. The one exception: if you're applying to, say, an engineering program that's considered part of a separate college, because in that case, you'll be part of a smaller pool of applicants. O'Neill says some schools may even ask what subject matter you'd like to study, then tailor their recruitment material to suit your interests. "We know that students might change their minds," he adds.

A variety of school and summer activities is impressive, especially if you've stuck with them for several years. Admissions officers notice if you sign up for 20 clubs during your senior year—and they aren't always impressed. O'Neill says our applicant's four years of high school cheerleading experience, for instance, show that she's "trustworthy and responsible"—especially because she was elected captain. Parker adds that it's obvious that she has initiative. "This is a girl who hasn't been lying on the beach," Parker says. "She's gotten internships."

Grades and Test Scores

One bad grade won't kill your chances to get into the school of your choice. Although our applicant was worried about a low math grade in her senior year, the experts got the full picture from her transcript and test scores. "She probably took more than she should have and the math class suffered," says O'Neill. Parker adds that grades are this student's strong point: "This is a girl who's taken seven AP classes and done superbly."

Extremely high SAT scores can win you points. Our News Teamer had a combined score of 1360, but Parker says that for most students applying to truly selective schools, "fourteen hundred is really an opening bid." By the way, he also discourages applicants from taking the tests too often. Take it twice, he advises—"no more, no less."

Essays and Recommendation Letters

"Silly" questions should be taken seriously. Although admissions folks often ask about your favorite musician, novel or motto to lighten up the application, these aren't throwaway opportunities to show off your witty irreverence. According to O'Neill, if the answers you give seem inappropriate or lightweight, admissions counselors may begin to question your seriousness overall. So if *The Animal* is your top movie, keep it to yourself.

Don't think admissions people expect you to come up with a plan to save the world. Questions that ask you to tackle major issues (homelessness, the AIDS epidemic) shouldn't be answered with a step-by-step proposal. "We're looking for thoughtfulness," says

> A variety of school and summer activities is impressive.

O'Neill. Instead of the unrealistic solution our applicant offered for this type of question, our experts prefer a more personal perspective on how the topic affects or concerns you. "A tip that I give kids is to be honest in their responses," says Parker.

If an application allows you to formulate your own question, write about something that is important to you. For example, you might want to discuss the reasons that Monet's *Water Lilies* is your favorite painting, or what news event truly devastated you. Don't make the mistake of rehashing your resume. As O'Neill says, it's hard to sound interesting while you're discussing your own stellar qualities. He'd like to see concrete evidence of your diligence or talent rather than a sentence saying "I'm gifted."

> Don't think admissions people expect you to come up with a plan to save the world.

Letters of recommendation from teachers are crucial. Although a letter from a *Teen People* editor helped our News Teamer's application, O'Neill gives more weight to what the faculty says. "I'd like to hear someone from school talk about her maturity. Those recs mean a lot to us," he says. So be nice to your teachers.

In most cases you won't be penalized for going to a small high school. According to Parker, what is important is that the applicant takes "full advantage" of the opportunities that his or her school has to offer. "We don't use a formula in this case," he says. "We have to interpret the setting the person is coming from." So if there are no advanced placement or international baccalaureate classes being offered at your high school, don't worry. You're not required to take any. . . .

Epilogue

OUR APPLICANT FILLS US IN ON THE OUTCOME OF HER COLLEGE SEARCH

When I first met with my guidance counselor, we discussed the fact that I had a real chance to get into some of the most competitive schools in the country. But he was honest with me. "Your SAT scores might give you some trouble," he said. Nevertheless—and with some trepidation—I decided to go ahead and try my luck at Harvard, Georgetown and Princeton. (I also applied to a few schools that I knew would probably accept me.) After months of anxiety, I got the news in April. Harvard rejected me. But I was accepted to Emory, Vanderbilt and the honors program at George Washington University—and was wait-listed at Georgetown and Princeton. Eventually Georgetown informed me that I'd been accepted, and that's where I just completed my freshman year. I'm glad that I took risks in my college search and, of course, I'm incredibly proud that my hard work in high school paid off!

Questions and Answers About College Application Essays

G. Gary Ripple

Many colleges require their applicants to write one or more personal essays. In the following selection, G. Gary Ripple makes up a dialogue between a "candidate" for college admission and a "dean" of admissions. The dean informs the candidate about what colleges are looking for in these essays and some common mistakes applicants make, such as being overly verbose or failing to check spelling. Ripple is director of admissions at Lafayette College in Pennsylvania and author of *Do-It Write: How to Prepare a Great College Application*, from which the following passage is excerpted.

Candidate: I'm stuck on these college essays! I haven't had this serious a case of writer's block since my sixth grade "What I did on my summer vacation" essay.

Dean: Welcome to the club. Remember—writing the essay is supposed to be a difficult task. Otherwise, every one would breeze right through it and no one would gain an advantage in the process of selection. Think of this as your big chance to rise above the crowd.

Candidate: Can you at least help me get started; give me a clue as to what you deans are looking for? Is this supposed to be a soap opera version of my life story, or a treatise on the meaning of life?

Dean: We want to meet the real you—someone other than a grade-point-average, an SAT score, and a class rank—a living, breathing human being who has both strengths and weaknesses. It is just as important for us to know the things you think need improvement in yourself as it is for us to know how you hope to strengthen our campus. Seriously, if you are already perfect, what can our college possibly do for you?

Candidate: Why am I having such a hard time finding the real me?

Dean: Like most of us, you spend a lot of time trying to be like everyone else, conforming to peer pressures. "Finding yourself" is a life-long (rewarding) battle, and now is a good time to start. You need only stop and ask yourself "How am I different from my friends and other classmates?"

Candidate: What if I say the wrong thing?

Dean: There are no right and wrong answers to a college essay question. No one who reads applicants' folders wants to think the freshman class will be filled by a bunch of docile conformists. No one has a particular personality trait he or she wants to purge from the student body. So you see, you can't lose—if you are honest about yourself.

Being Honest

Candidate: What do you mean "honest"?

Dean: I mean realistic about who you are and who you are not. Believe me, we can spot "phony" all the way across a room full of folders, sort of like how Santa knows who's been good and who's been bad. We also know when someone else (especially a parent) is responsible for the answers. Write the essays yourself and never allow yourself to be misrepresented by anyone, including yourself.

Candidate: Are there any essay topics I should avoid?

Dean: Try not to use a topic that is on everyone's mind. Recent blockbuster movies or an all consuming world-wide problem (e.g., the battle to eliminate HIV) will overburden admission officers giving them so many seemingly identical essays that the effectiveness of each is seriously lessened. Also, try to avoid life histories, trendy causes, ways to save the world (unless you're asked specifically), and lengthy analyses of romantic relationships. *Remember, the best essay is one which only you could write!*

> There are no right and wrong answers to a college essay question.

Candidate: Do I have to worry that my answers will ever come back to haunt me? Will I one day find them published in a book like this?

Dean: Of course not. The admission process is a relatively private one and the answers you provide are meant only to assist the readers in their evaluation of your record. Is this institution the place for you to continue your growth and development? Nothing you say on an application form can ever come back to haunt you as long as it is a truthful representation of who you are at that point in time. It is only a snapshot, not a long-running motion picture.

Candidate: How long should the essay be?

Dean: Only as long as necessary to make your point. Avoid overly verbose responses. Say your piece as concisely and economically as possible and don't worry about the length (unless, of course, the application requests a specific length; then, follow those instructions exactly).

Candidate: What are some of the big mistakes people make?

Dean: For one, they frequently start writing their answer before they have carefully read the question and all of the directions provided. Try to imagine how you would react, as a selection committee member, to an answer written by someone who obviously had not read (or understood) the question or the directions. Is this the kind of student you would want at your college? No. At best, it indicates carelessness; more likely, it indicates a lesser level of literacy.

Secondly, a number of people mistakenly attempt to stretch their vocabulary by using words with which they are not entirely comfortable. They forget that some of the best writing of all time has been done in one and two syllables (think of the poetry of Dr. Seuss), so please don't worry about using big words in an application essay. It's more important that you use the "correct" word and demonstrate an appreciation for the nuances of vocabulary.

Another common mistake is the failure to check spelling. Don't rely on "spellchecker" software; it misses a lot, and as long as there is a proofreader left in this world, you have no excuse for submitting an application full of misspelled words or typographical errors. . . .

Candidate: Can I change anything after my application has been mailed? You never know, I may win the Nobel prize, and . . .

Dean: Of course. If you win the Nobel prize, we certainly want to know about it. You should, however, make certain your original answers are thoroughly considered, and only make changes if you believe they will have a significant impact on our admission decision. Just clearly identify yourself as a previous applicant and the author of any additional work submitted. If a school has placed you on a waiting list for admission, then you may wish to consider sending in supplemental material if something has occurred since you filed your original application. This will encourage the admission committee to reopen your file and take a fresh look at you as an applicant. It also demonstrates the seriousness of your interest in being considered a candidate for admission.

How Your Guidance Counselor Can Help

Rachel Hartigan Shea

In this article, Rachel Hartigan Shea, a staff reporter for *U.S. News & World Report*, tells high school students that their guidance counselors are important resources for getting admitted into college. Guidance counselors not only write recommendations for college applications, but often become a student's advocate by pleading his or her case before college admissions officials. Shea recommends that students take the initiative to meet with the counselors at their own school.

Far too many high schoolers end up navigating college admissions with little help from the guidance office. Why? The numbers tell the story. Although experts recommend that the student-to-counselor ratio in a school not exceed 250 to 1, at big public high schools the ratio can push as high as 565 to 1. Not only do most counselors have too many students, they also have too many duties, including scheduling classes, finding resources for learning-disabled students, and dealing with troublemakers.

But don't even think about avoiding your harried counselor. Counselors write the recommendations that, come April of your

Rachel Hartigan Shea, "Getting Good Guidance," *U.S. News & World Report*, September 12, 2001, p. 93. Copyright © 2001 by U.S. News & World Report, Inc. Reproduced by permission.

senior year, help determine whether you receive fat envelopes or skinny ones. If they visit a lot of campuses and are plugged into the college admissions scene, they probably speak regularly with admissions officers about individual applicants. They may even tell them who they think are the best candidates from their school. Sometimes "I will hand write a note [to an admissions officer] if I think a student is a particularly good match," admits Shirley Bloomquist, until recently director of guidance at Thomas Jefferson High School for Science and Technology in Alexandria, V.A.

Special Help

And if you are turned down everywhere you apply, your counselor might even plead your case on a national listserv [electronic mailing list] to admissions officials at schools that still have open slots.

These are people you definitely want watching your back, so don't be shy about making the first move. Pop into your counselor's office to talk about college, extracurriculars, and the state of the world in general. If your counselor is too swamped for frequent chats, drop off a resume that lists your recent accomplishments for her file. "If students are going to brag to anyone, we're the people," says Risa Green, codirector of college counseling at Milken Community High School in Los Angeles.

> These are people you definitely want watching your back, so don't be shy about making the first move.

While your counselor is getting to know you, get to know your counselor's resources. Ask for a tour of the guidance office, and if your school hosts workshops on college admissions, attend every one and sit in the front row.

What if your counselor resists all advances or simply doesn't know enough about colleges to be helpful? Try making an appointment with another counselor at your school. If your school won't allow you to officially switch, consider hiring an independent counselor. But be warned that high school counselors can't be entirely evaded—they still write the recommendations.

Never fear, though. College admissions committees know that, for various reasons, not everyone receives adequate counseling or a fair recommendation. Says Karen Long, associate dean of admissions at Colgate University in Hamilton, N.Y., "We try not to hold [a mediocre letter] against a candidate if the rest of an application is strong."

Is Early Decision for You?

Constance Faye Mudore

Most colleges that do not have open or rolling admissions policies send letters of acceptance or rejection to applicants in March or April; students then have until May 1 to decide which college they wish to enroll in. However, some schools have instituted an "Early Decision" (E.D.) option for applicants. As described in the following article by Constance Faye Mudore, Early Decision requires that students submit their applications to the college of their choice early in their senior year of high school and agree to attend that college if they are accepted (notifications are generally made in December). Mudore reports that more and more high school students are considering E.D. because it increases their chances of being accepted by competitive schools. However, the author points out, many counselors and educators believe some students using the E.D. option are making commitments before they are ready. Another disadvantage of E.D. is that students are unable to weigh financial aid offers from competing schools. Mudore is a writer for *Current Health* and other publications for young people.

For Kelly Keegan, it was love at first sight. "I visited lots of schools in Pennsylvania, but the minute I walked on the campus at Gettysburg College, I knew I wanted to come here." She was impressed by the layout of the campus, the small student-teacher ratio, and the school's strong political science program. But mostly, she liked how the school felt. Says Keegan, "I knew I'd be unhappy anywhere else."

Kelly's confidence that Gettysburg was the right school prompted her to apply there for Early Decision, one of several early application options offered by many schools. Could Early Decision be for you?

One Size Does Not Fit All

In order to answer that question, let's consider a number of admissions options generally offered by four-year colleges and universities.

• *Regular Admission.* This is the most common option. Students apply by the middle of winter and are notified whether or not they are accepted by early April. They have until May 1 to respond.

• *Rolling Admission.* Students apply and find out whether or not they are admitted within four to six weeks of application. The school accepts students who meet admissions criteria on a first-come, first-served basis until all spaces are filled.

• *Open Admission.* Almost all high school graduates who apply are admitted until no more space is available.

Many guidance counselors . . . are concerned about the trend toward hopping on the early application bandwagon.

Early options include:

• *Early Admission.* A student with exceptional ability is admitted before completing high school.

• *Early Decision.* A student declares a first-choice college, submits an application by October 1, and requests that the school decide on admission by January 1. The student agrees to attend the school if admitted, and to relinquish the right to wait until May 1 to decide.

• *Early Action.* This is similar to Early Decision, but the student is not obligated to attend the school if admitted and can wait until May 1 to respond.

Growing Popularity

Even though early application options have been around for a while, they have grown a lot more popular in recent years. This increased popularity has generated controversy, especially in regard to Early Decision (also known as E.D.) and its binding nature.

How popular have early action options become? Consider Harvard. For the freshman class entering in the fall of 2001, the school offered 2,041 students admission. Of those, 1,101—approximately 54 percent—were Early Action.

Other schools are also reporting increases in early option admissions ranging between 25 and 33 percent. Marlyn McGrath Lewis, director of admissions at Harvard, told the *Princeton Review*, "The competition of college admissions recently reached a sort of legendary difficulty status in which applying early was thought to give people an edge." She says the idea then became contagious.

And in fact, according to the College Board, a growing number of colleges and universities are adding early plans to their timelines. So, if early application is a growing trend, why not just do it?

Many guidance counselors and college admissions officers are concerned about the trend toward hopping on the early application bandwagon. They believe that E.D. in particular may force students to make college decisions before they're ready.

According to Scott Flanagan, dean of admissions and financial aid at Edgewood College in Madison, Wisconsin, "Only after students have conducted a thorough college search and are

The Difference in Acceptance Rates, Based on SAT Scores

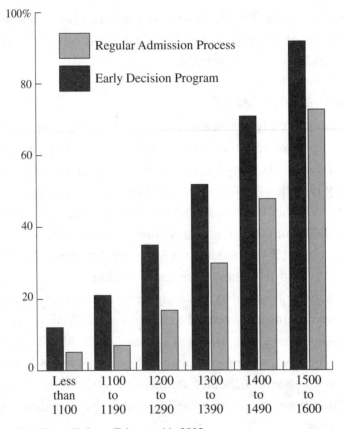

New York Times Upfront, February 11, 2002.

positive that they have found the 'perfect' school should they consider Early Decision."

The Pros

What are the advantages of applying under Early Decision? E.D. helps reduce the anxiety of waiting for a decision until spring of your senior year. In addition, it can eliminate the time and expense of sending applications to lots of schools.

Applying under E.D. may help your chances of getting into a school, since you are competing against fewer applicants. (Typically, the number of students who apply E.D. is less than the number applying under regular admission.) Another plus is that when you apply E.D., you're letting a school know that it is your top choice, which may boost your admission prospects.

The Cons

One of the strongest arguments against E.D. is that it can be tough to back out if you change your mind. Early Decision is a legally binding arrangement between you and a college. Once you are accepted, you sign an agreement that you will withdraw all applications you have made to other schools. If you don't keep your promise to attend the college after being granted Early Decision admission, other schools can refuse to admit you.

Clemence Sullivan, a freshman at Carleton College in Northfield, Minnesota, did not apply under Early Decision because of its binding nature. Sullivan says, "Senior year of high school, you really grow and change. What looked good in October may not look as good to you in the spring. I wanted to keep my options open."

Early Decision is so binding that the only way you can get released is if the school doesn't help meet your financial needs. Financial need is not the same as your family's willingness to pay, however. Need is determined by federal and school formulas applied to the income and asset information you and your parents supply on a financial aid application.

> One of the strongest arguments against E.D. is that it can be tough to back out if you change your mind.

And speaking of money, there is also the argument that since E.D. locks students in, there's not much incentive for a school to give an applicant a great financial aid package. Unfortunately, students who have applied E.D., or to only one school, don't have the financial aid offers of other colleges to bargain for a better deal.

The Best Decision

Early Decision is not a shortcut to college admission. Selecting the right school involves finding the one that most closely fits as many of your interests as possible. E.D. doesn't eliminate the self-exploration necessary to determine what those interests are. Nor does it reduce the need to explore several schools so that you can compare and determine the best match.

If you *have* found your one dream school and are ready to commit to Early Decision, that's fine. But if not, that's all right, too. The college admissions process isn't a race. Give yourself enough time to explore all your options. That way, early or not, you'll make the best decision for *you*.

Chapter 4

Alternatives to the Four-Year College

Choosing Not to Go to College

Betsy Rubiner

Not all people benefit from four years in college, nor do they need a college degree in order to succeed in work or in life, writes Betsy Rubiner. In fact, there are many good jobs available that do not require a bachelor's degree, she writes. However, this does not necessarily mean that teens can forgo education after high school. Many jobs require a solid high school education *and* some form of vocational training or education that is available through community colleges or technical institutes. Rubiner is a freelance writer who specializes in writing about children and families. Her work has appeared in the *New York Times* and other publications.

True, going to college for four years can be an enriching, eye-opening experience. True, a bachelor's degree is still an asset if you're trying to make it in America. It's also a must for many créme de la crème careers.

But not all kids are cut out for college, despite the expectations of their parents or teachers. And, especially in the brave new world of the 21st century, not all kids need to go to college right after high school—or ever—to succeed, says J. Michael Farr, author of *America's Top Jobs for People Without a Four-Year Degree.*

"The mythology here is that everybody has to go to college to do well. Not true," says Farr. "This generation is a little bit better off than ours. But there are so many more options. It's more complex now."

New Opportunities

A boom economy coupled with dramatic changes in technology have created entirely new jobs and expanded opportunities in age-old professions. Many of these occupations—from computer programmers and Web page designers to chefs and police officers—don't require a bachelor's degree. Neither do many good jobs in the arts, crafts, skilled trades, construction, service industry, science, and health fields. Such jobs include: aircraft mechanic, cardiovascular technologist, electronic technician, law clerk, registered nurse, sales rep, secretary, travel agent . . . the list goes on.

Jenna Norvell, 21, is now full of career ideas thanks to a ten-month cosmetology program she attended this year [2000] at the Aveda Institute in Minneapolis. She paid $9,865 for tuition and about $6,000 more in expenses, including rent for a one-bedroom apartment she shared with another student. Although Norvell got lots of career leads from salon recruiters at a career fair hosted by the institute, she didn't meet any from California—where she wants to live. So she plans to find a job out West on her own, perhaps in television or maybe doing makeup for fashion shows. Or selling cosmetics. Or managing a salon. "You'd be surprised how many occupations there are in this field," says Norvell.

> In the brave new world of the 21st century, not all kids need to go to college right after high school—or ever—to succeed.

High school students often don't understand there are so many options available to them, says Farr. "That's a shame. People who are interested in various things really can earn a decent living even if they don't want to go to college."

Percentage of High School Completers Who Were Enrolled in College the October After Completing High School, by Family Income: 1976, 1986, and 1996

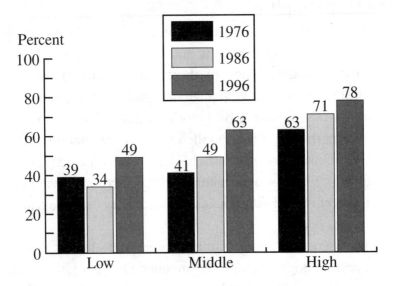

*Low income is the bottom 20 percent of all families; high income is the top 20 percent; and middle income is the 60 percent in between.

U.S. Department of Commerce, Bureau of the Census, Current Population Survey, October (various years).

It's still true that people with more education, on average, earn more money. But 28 percent of workers without a four-year degree earn more than the average worker with a bachelor's degree, according to Harlow G. Unger, author of *But What if I Don't Want to Go to College?*, a guide to educational alternatives to college. And more and more computer-savvy young people are skipping college to join the high-tech revolution as computer network engineers, Internet entrepreneurs, and game designers.

Don't get the wrong idea. This doesn't mean you can waltz right into a great job straight out of high school with no skills, training, or effort. To get a good job without a four-year degree, you still must have at least a solid high school education. "Even if you think you're not going to college, you still need to pay attention," says Farr. "You need to know how to be part of a team, how to communicate effectively verbally, how to learn."

Vocational Training

And chances are, you will need training after high school through some form of alternative career education. Only four of the fastest growing occupations in the United States require a four-year degree or more, says Unger. But many of the others—home health aides, building maintenance, teaching aides—require post-high-school training.

Which vocational education and training you'll need—and the cost—depends upon the vocation you choose. Public community colleges offer some of the best vocational training, often specializing in areas such as the graphic arts, hotel and restaurant management, and building trades, according to Unger. Full-time tuition averages $1,200 a year, although the range from state-to-state is $600 to $3,500. Vocational training at technical institutes will be costlier. Private junior colleges average $7,000 a year, according to Unger. Tuition for private-for-profit trade schools that usually specialize in one field, such as hair-styling or auto mechanics, varies widely, and Unger warns students to be wary of unethical operators.

Not just any vocational education or training will do. The trick is to find reputable, high-quality programs and to avoid con artists and dead-end programs, advises Unger. Look for programs that are accredited, offer in-depth academic and vocational instruction, teach real skills for real jobs, provide hands-on work experience, help students in job-hunting, and are linked to potential employers.

Too often, Unger argues, parents push their reluctant children to go to college. Many drop out. "We are forcing hundreds of thousands of kids to go to college and they clearly do not want to be there," he says.

What High School Students Can Do

What about high school graduates who don't want college and don't know what to do next? Start by visiting your school guidance office or library to thumb through *The Occupational Outlook Handbook* published every two years by the U.S. Labor Department. It offers nuts-and-bolts descriptions of jobs and the training required.

Think about what interests you—sports, music, gardening, whatever—and what jobs let you pursue that interest, advises Unger. Visit people who do these jobs. Ask questions.

For example, a high school graduate who loves animals might find a great job grooming dogs in a kennel. But she may outgrow the grooming job. That day, she may decide to go to college to become a veterinarian. "A lot of kids who say they don't want to go to college wind up going anyway, later on," says Unger.

A Detour Before College

Tracey Randinelli

Some students, writes Tracey Randinelli, are not ready to step into college right after high school. Randinelli, a freelance writer and frequent contributor to *Careers & Colleges* magazine, examines some of the choices young people have. Many of these choices involve postponing college to pursue travel, work, or other experiences. Students should not be afraid to explore all of these options, including those that do not involve college right away, Randinelli concludes.

As the summer of 1999 came to a close, most of Carla Brown's high school friends were packing stereos and bean bag chairs for their college dorm rooms. Brown was packing something else: a passport. The graduate of Milton Academy in Massachusetts, was bound for London to intern with a humanitarian group that raises money for conservation efforts in Madagascar. She had already spent the summer as an au pair in Italy. And she followed up her London stint with nearly six months in New Zealand, doing everything from assisting a commercial photographer to taking care of the feathered residents of a bird sanctuary. When she returned to the States the next summer, Brown was eager to start her studies at Oberlin College in

Ohio. "I came back with a new attitude," she says. "I was really excited to be learning."

When it comes to getting a higher education, some students, like Brown, aren't ready to jump directly into college. The U.S. Department of Education reports that more than 30 percent of female high school graduates and about 40 percent of male grads haven't enrolled in college within a year of graduating from high school. And many of those who do enroll aren't quite ready, which may explain why one-third of college freshmen don't return to school for their sophomore year, according to *The Chronicle of Higher Education*.

> Many . . . [college students] aren't quite ready, which may explain why one-third of college freshmen don't return to school for their sophomore year.

As high school wraps up, you might want to consider some of the options—taking time off to travel, pursuing an interest or hobby, working, studying at a community college or technical school, or joining the military.

A Year Off

Although she had been accepted to Oberlin, Carla Brown decided to defer her admission. "I felt pretty tired of schoolwork," she says. "I'd been going to school since I was five. I needed to have a time in my life that was completely separate from academics, to do something I wanted to do."

Linda Lee, author of *Success Without College* says that some students are simply tired of the whole grind of reading, writing, and arithmetic. "By the time they finish their senior year, it's not just a mild case of *senioritis*," says Lee. "These kids have had it. They want to figure out who they are without someone grading them."

In many areas of the world, it's customary to spend the year after high school graduation traveling or participating in a community service or work program. The idea may be catching on in the U.S. as well. A growing number of opportunities are available for students who want to take some time off. Some ideas:

- *ENVIRONMENTAL PROGRAM:* Gets you outdoors (usually on a volunteer basis), working to save some aspect of the planet.
- *CULTURAL IMMERSION PROGRAM:* You live in another country for a period of time, learning the language and customs of the area.
- *APPRENTICESHIP:* Gives you hands-on training from an expert in a trade—everything from marble cutting to electronics.
- *INTERNSHIP:* An entry-level, temporary job that allows you to learn more about the field.
- *COMMUNITY SERVICE:* Your hard work helps improve the lives of others and may teach you new skills.

One thing is clear: Taking a year off isn't for those looking to make big bucks. In fact, many interim programs can cost as much as a year at a private university. The trick to lowering the cost, says Bob Gilpin, president of Where You Headed (www.whereyouheaded.com), an educational consulting firm, is to be flexible in your requirements.

> In many areas of the world, it's customary to spend the year after high school graduation traveling or participating in a community service . . . program.

"Say you want to apprentice with a glass blower or work with someone developing software," he says. "The likelihood of being able to do that inexpensively is very good" as long as you take what the program offers without making demands about the location, the timing, etc.

In other programs, you pay not with cash, but with time and hard work. "You might have to drive a bus back and forth from camp every week," Gilpin explains. "You won't earn money, but you'll get a place to stay and stuff to eat." At one point during her trip through New Zealand, Carla Brown took a position at a conservation organization "in return for a place to sleep."

Work

During her senior year at H.D. Woodson High School in Washington, D.C., Carmen Harris decided to put off college in favor of a full-time job with the Red Cross, first as an administrative assistant, then with the marketing department. "I took a business track in high school and knew I really liked it," she explains. A year and a half later, she enrolled in Washington's Strayer University with a newfound passion—marketing, and she still held down a full-time job.

> The job opportunities for a student fresh out of high school are not limited to flipping burgers.

As Harris's experience proves, the job opportunities for a student fresh out of high school are not limited to flipping burgers. Getting a good job is all about being thorough and diligent: putting together a detailed résumé, networking, and approaching an interview in a professional manner. "If a kid puts as much effort into getting a job as he or she would in applying to college," says Linda Lee, "he or she should get something better than minimum wage."

The trick is to market the skills you have that are most enticing to employers. For many students, those skills involve computers. "I had a lot of computer skills on my résumé; a lot of experience I had gotten from summer jobs," says Harris. "It was pretty easy for me to get a foot in the door that way."

A job may even earn you more than money. In many cases, a job that introduces you to subjects and career opportunities you find interesting can be the catalyst you need to start college. Harris found that her co-workers motivated her. "There were a lot of adults going back to school and talking about what they were studying," she says. "They were encouraging me, and finally I was like, 'If they're ready, I'm ready.'"

Military Service

It's a big jump from would-be professional flutist to Navy recruit, but it's one Susan Raddant made a year after graduating from Shawano High School in Wisconsin. Raddant originally planned to enter the music conservatory at Lawrence University in Appleton, Wisconsin, but was lacking two things: funds and motivation. "I didn't have the discipline and the focus to know what I wanted to do with my life," she says. "I was a small town girl—I needed some experience."

Partly influenced by the advice of her brother-in-law, a Navy recruiter, Raddant joined up and eventually found herself stationed in Iceland and working in military journalism. After three-and-a-half years in Iceland and two more in Portugal, Raddant returned to the U.S. and finally entered Lawrence University—eight years after she graduated from high school!

Because of her military work with foreign embassies, she ended up studying government and international studies at Lawrence. She's now preparing for a diplomatic job with the U.S. State Department.

If, like Raddant, you have a hankering to see the world, you may want to investigate the United States military. After basic training, you receive instruction in a specific field. Once you've completed your enlistment, which can take several years, you can opt to stay or use the skills you've developed to find a job in the civilian world.

According to Jim Rapp, a 26-year-old who graduated from Illinois State University in Normal after spending two years in the Marines, military experience can be beneficial when job-hunting. "Human resources people look at me and say, 'He's proven himself by being in the military and going to college,'" he says.

One of the biggest benefits of military service: If you decide to go to college after finishing a military stint, the U.S. government will pick up a good portion of the tab.

The main drawback? Once you enlist, there's no turning back. "You belong to the government," says Larry Fowler, a former Navy SEAL and president of ArmedForcesCareers.com. "If there's a war and you're told to charge, you have to charge"—a fact that makes the decision-making process critical. Fowler suggests visiting a base for the weekend to determine if military life is really for you.

Community College

When financial difficulties forced Amanda Lents to work for a year after high school and then attend Monroe Community College in Rochester, New York, she was unhappy. "My friends thought I was throwing away my life," she says. "They, like I, were under the impression that a community college was for dropouts. We were all very wrong."

Lents, now 24, made an important discovery: Whether it's an alternative or a first step to a four-year school, a community college education has a lot to offer. Community colleges cost significantly less than four-year schools, and usually offer varied hours for students with full-time jobs. "Many of our students don't have the luxury of postponing work and going to school full time," says Dr. Antonio Perez, president of the Borough of Manhattan Community College in New York City.

> If . . . you have a hankering to see the world, you may want to investigate the United States military.

In addition, community colleges give students who are unsure of what they want to do a chance to try new things and experiment without a huge financial sacrifice. And because class sizes are often smaller than at a large university, students tend to get more one-on-one time with professors. "Community colleges are dedicated to teaching and not so much to research," explains Dr. Carmelita Thomas, president of the Western Campus at Cuyahoga Community College in Cleveland. "The faculty's level of education is equivalent to that of a university faculty, but they are working more closely with students."

> Many adults—and . . . parents—don't think putting off college to do something else with your life is a bad idea.

What that means is that students who choose to attend a community college are in good shape if they decide to transfer to a four-year school. For many students, an associate degree from a community college is enough to land them a great job. "We have degrees in computer science that put students in very well-paying jobs immediately—$40,000 to $50,000 a year."

Lents credits her associate degree from Monroe—not the bachelor's she later earned at Ithaca College—with preparing her for her television career (she's worked as a production assistant on *Diagnosis Murder* and *Whose Line Is It Anyway?*). "The professors [at Ithaca] had nothing to teach me that I hadn't learned at community college for a quarter of the price."

Technical College

Marco Correia's post–high school plans didn't include college. But that didn't mean he wasn't going on to school. After traveling to Portugal to visit relatives the summer following graduation, Correia returned home to Hartford, Connecticut, and worked with his father's dry cleaning and laundromat business for a few months. Then, in the spring, he entered New England Technical Institute in New Britain, Connecticut, to study Heating Ventilation Air Conditioning (HVAC). He'll be finished with classes—and hopefully apprenticing—by next spring. "Even junior year in high school, I knew I didn't want to go to college," says Correia, 19. "Tech college involves working with my hands, and that's what I've always liked to do."

A technical college (also called vo-tech or trade school) mixes school and work to give you the entry-level skills you need to begin a specific trade or occupation—usually one that's hands-on. There are tech colleges for hundreds of fields—culinary arts, secretarial, cosmetology, electronic, dental hygiene, legal assisting, broadcasting—as well as schools that encompass several different trades. When you're finished, you normally receive a certification rather than a diploma. After that, you usually receive more hands-on training in a job or apprentice situation before becoming licensed in the field.

The Final Word

Whatever you decide to do after high school, it's important to talk to people familiar with the decision-making process you're experiencing. Don't be afraid to explore all the options—including those that don't necessarily involve college right away. "There's no bad grade for going to a guidance counselor and asking what happens if I don't go," says Linda Lee.

And it might surprise you to hear that many adults—and many parents—don't think putting off college to do something else with your life is a bad idea. "It's the ideal time to do it. They don't have debts, they don't have families," says Lee. "What better time than at 18 to go out and find out who you are and if you can function outside your family?"

Taking Time Off for Volunteer Work

Colin Hall and Ron Lieber

One option high school students might consider instead of going straight to college is to take a year or more after high school for volunteer work or community service. The following selection tells the story of one such student, Cory Mason, who decided not to go to college immediately after high school but instead volunteered for Habitat for Humanity, a charitable organization that builds homes for low-income families. His experience proved a valuable education in itself. Mason was one of several students profiled in the book *Taking Time Off* by authors Colin Hall and Ron Lieber.

W hile Cory Mason's friends were busily filling out college applications, he was on the way to setting a record for skipping the most days of school and still graduating.

Cory had begun high school full of enthusiasm, lettering on the varsity swim team as a freshman and eventually qualifying for swim nationals. "Any self-discipline I've ever had comes from swimming," Cory observed. "Practice is grueling: you go back and forth over and over again. There's no change of scenery, and you can't really talk to anybody."

Cory attended a public high school in Racine, Wisconsin, with 2,400 students. He was in the international baccalaureate [IB] program, which he described as "almost a school within a school." IB programs usually consist of an accelerated work-intensive course of study for talented students, and they can be found in many countries. "Out of six hundred kids in my graduating class," Cory said, "fifty were in the IB program. We had the best teachers in each department, which was an unfair advantage, but we had a lot more homework, too."

Early on in high school, many of Cory's friends came from swimming. "There were three or four of us who got on the varsity level freshman year. That was great, but they hazed the hell out of us. One time they tied up one of my friends naked in a towel bag, threw him into the pool during girls' swim class, and when he got out of the bag, there he was, stark naked. It was awful."

Because of the swim meets he participated in every weekend, the Mason family could no longer go to church on Sundays. "Sometimes we'd go fifteen weekends in a row where we'd be at swim meets every weekend. It consumed our entire life. My dad looked at that time the family spent together as our church. He firmly believed that religion didn't necessarily have to take place in church, and he was glad that his family was together and that his kids were doing something constructive."

Swimming started to wear on Cory at the end of high school, and a shoulder injury increased his ambivalence about the sport. "It dawned on me, was it really worth it to work hard seven months at a crack, without a break, in order to drop my time by half a second?

Like all his friends, Cory went through the motions of applying to colleges during his senior year.

"I went through a period where I just felt real blasé about everything. It drove my parents up the wall. Some people at my school went through a senior slump; I had a senior plummet. The last two years of high school seemed to last forever. I wanted to be grownup and have real responsibilities."

Like all his friends, Cory went through the motions of applying to colleges during his senior year. As the time approached to make a decision, however, he became certain that going straight to college was not for him. "It just seemed that everybody I knew was going to the University of Wisconsin at Madison. A lot of kids from my school go there and only hang out with the kids they knew from high school. That just seems so limiting, and I was really scared that was going to happen to me."

> Cory's duties . . . included helping build houses, overseeing and managing the construction sites, and training the volunteers.

In the midst of a difficult senior year, Cory also was going through a year-long confirmation program with his priest, Father Bruce. "Father Bruce was really cool; he's the only priest I know who wears an earring. The main group met on Sunday nights and we had a smaller group that met on Tuesday nights to discuss things in greater depth.

"Our small group studied the vow of nonviolence, not just physical violence, but also violence of the heart and mind. We are in a society that is constantly bombarded with violence. Our entire legal system is adversarial; our political system is confrontational. I was learning more through confirmation than I was in school."

Cory's confirmation program also included community service. "During Christmas, we were each given a family that we had to raise money for. We organized a Polar Bear plunge. We ran into Lake Michigan on January 14. The water was freezing, and they had an ambulance on hand. A couple of us were crazy enough to swim out to the buoy and back. We got on the front page of the newspaper. It's now become a tradition, and we bring in a couple thousand dollars every year."

Cory recalls telling Father Bruce that he was not ready to go to college. "I had heard so many stories about the kids at Madison. They go up there, party all the time, don't go to class, and flunk out their first semester. What a waste. And I tell you, that would have been me."

When Cory asked Father Bruce if he knew anything about missionary work, Father Bruce gave him some booklets. Unfortunately, many of the organizations only wanted people who were at least twenty-one years old. "You would think, with something like missionary work, that when someone asks to volunteer they'd do everything they could to encourage that person and help him or her set it up. It was the most bureaucratic thing I've ever been involved with."

Cory's parents wondered what he was doing. "I had to explain to them why we had this astronomical phone bill, including calls to Venezuela. I told them I was thinking about taking time off and investigating the possibilities of some kind of religiously inspired community service in South America. My dad said, 'Cory, I know so many kids that took time off and never came back. It's rough out there in the real world.' I said, 'Yeah, yeah, you're right,' but with my mom, who knew I was not ready for college, I convinced him to give me the benefit of the doubt."

Cory applied to work for Habitat for Humanity and was accepted in June. Habitat for Humanity is an organization dedicated to providing affordable housing for low-income families. Habitat now has affiliates in forty-five countries, with close to 1,200 chapters in the United States.

Habitat gave Cory a choice of three sites: Ontario, Canada; Waco, Texas; and Savannah, Georgia. "I decided on Savannah because they let me be project manager, and the fact that it was ten miles away from the ocean was real appealing. The town is beautiful, right on the Savannah River."

Cory's duties as project manager included helping build houses, overseeing and managing the construction sites, and training the volunteers and recipient families. In return for his services, he was given room, board, and a stipend of $20 a week.

"It was rough getting by on $20 a week," he said. "And if you wanted to use the truck, you had to put gas in it. It was an old beat-up Chevy truck that gets something like eight miles to the gallon, and you had to drive all the way into town and all the way back."

Cory was in charge of a project to build fifty-two new houses on a thirteen-acre site in rural Savannah. "I had never built a house before, nor had I lifted a hammer to do anything aside from hang a picture on a wall." But Cory caught on quickly. He figured out a lot on his own, and he also had two teachers—the other project manager at his site, and a construction superintendent hired by Habitat.

Habitat builds houses which vary in size, depending on the size of the recipient family, with an average of 1,500 square feet per home. The houses come with heat and central air, a stove, and a refrigerator. Habitat sells the houses for approximately $30,000, an affordable price achieved through private donations of money, labor, and materials.

Recipient families chosen by a Habitat committee are required to put five hundred hours of "sweat equity" into the house. They then buy the house with a no-interest mortgage which can be paid back over the course of fifteen to twenty-five years.

> Cory found it inspiring to work with people from varied backgrounds.

"Working for Habitat was a real eye-opening experience," Cory explained. "There are families in America who are living in Third World conditions. Unfortunately, charity is usually directed to the so-called deserving poor in our country, those people who have jobs and are trying to make a go of it. Meanwhile, we call the poor people most in need of assistance 'undeserving' and ignore them.

"I heard a social worker give a speech in Savannah called 'Standing Next to Pain,' and he said that it was important to try and walk in other people's shoes. He said, 'Look, everybody's got pain, but in addition to the pain of being alive, which we all share—becoming sick and losing loved ones—the poor are stricken with the pain of poverty.'"

When to Take Time Off

If you are still in high school, you should go through the college application process, choose a school, and then ask that school to defer your admission until the following year. Most colleges will be happy to oblige, and this will be a big relief to your family. It will also take pressure off you, because it is more difficult to apply to college when you are not in school and the resources of your college counselor are not immediately available. If you are in college already when you decide to leave, speak to a dean and make sure that a place will be waiting for you when you return.

Some people will warn you that you will be behind your peers when you come back. If they tell you this before you go to college, don't believe them. One year makes little material difference in the broad scheme of things, and the fact that your best friend from high school may graduate from college twelve months earlier than you will seem less significant as time goes by. If they are telling you that you will be behind your peers while you are *in* college, they may have a point. Taking time off after junior year in college and then returning to find all your friends already graduated can be difficult.

Colin Hall and Ron Lieber, *Taking Time Off*, 1996.

Cory found it inspiring to work with people from varied backgrounds. "The thing about working construction is, nobody wears nice clothes. People would show up in jeans and T-shirts. Most of the rich people who volunteered from the nearby retirement community didn't know much about construction, and neither did most of the recipients. That was one of the neatest things about working there; seeing people from all different walks of life coming together and deciding they were going to put up a wall that afternoon."

The most difficult part of Cory's stay in Savannah came toward the end of February. "Habitat International had what's called the Spring Break Challenge. They go to college campuses and recruit groups to work at a site for a week. I was a little worried about telling these twenty-two-year-olds what to do. I thought they were going to say, 'You're just a little punk out of high school. What are you talking about?' But when it came right down to it, most of them had no clue about construction, and I did."

"We went forty-three days straight without a day off. It was rough, because at night in the dormitories they'd say, 'We want to see what Savannah's like, can you show us around the town?' By the time I left, I could have applied to be a tour guide for the summer."

> "I see kids in college who could be learning a lot more by just taking a year off and working somewhere."

When Cory left Savannah, he was able to get a job working construction in Racine. "It was great, because I was learning a trade. I learned all about roofing, Sheetrock, electricity, and a little bit about plumbing."

After working in Racine for the summer, Cory enrolled at Centenary College, a small Methodist-affiliated liberal-arts school in Shreveport, Louisiana.

"Coming back to Racine was good. I had been at odds with my parents when I was living at home my senior year. When I came back, they were actually glad to have me. Earlier, my dad had been kind of worried. His oldest son, who was supposed to go off to college, was doing something kind of wacky. But by the time I left for Centenary, he was actually proud of what I had done and would tell people at work about it.

"For a long time, I took great pride in being discontent with everything around me. There was a certain appeal to that, being a pain in the ass. That's not to say that I don't still question things that go on around me. The biggest change, though, is that now I'm at peace with myself.

"I see kids in college who could be learning a lot more by just taking a year off and working somewhere. You learn to pay your bills. You have to make sure you know where your next meal is coming from. You also learn that if you don't have an education you can't get a stable job. I didn't like scraping by on $20 a week, and I don't want to scrape for my next meal the rest of my life.

"You can't learn that without leaving school. In college, you just live in your dorm room, all your meals are cooked for you, and it's pretty simple. All you have to do is show up."

Community Colleges

Pat Ordovensky

The two-year or community college is the fastest-growing segment of American education, writes Pat Ordovensky, and is an option that many students should consider. He provides a list of reasons why community colleges may be the best education alternative after high school, including convenience, low cost, and a varied curriculum. People who earn an associate degree at a community college can often transfer to a four-year institution to earn a bachelor's degree. Ordovensky, the author of *College Planning for Dummies* (excerpted here), was an education writer for *USA Today*.

Right now, about 6 million students are attending two-year colleges. Can 6 million students be wrong?

The two-year college—known in various places as a community college, junior college, or technical college—is the fastest growing segment of education at any level, kindergarten through Ph.D. Almost half of today's college students took their first college course on a two-year campus.

As you make your lists seeking your right colleges, the two-year option certainly is worth a glance. A two-year school may be your safety valve school. Such a school may turn out to be

Pat Ordovensky, "(Almost) Ten Reasons Why a Two-Year College Is Worth a Look," *College Planning for Dummies*, Foster City, CA: IDG Books, 1999. Copyright © 1999 by Pat Ordovensky. Reproduced by permission.

your college of choice. This chapter lists reasons you should think about attending a two-year college.

Convenience

Almost everyone in the United States (except in very rural areas) is within a 30-minute drive of a two-year college. Most people are even closer. Every state now operates some kind of community college system and tries to put a campus in every decently populated county.

Getting to a community college is like driving to a grocery store. You get in the car, go, park, attend classes for a couple hours, and drive home. Your expenses are a gallon of gas and, maybe, a buck to park. That's convenient.

Plus, almost all two-year colleges offer a large portion of their classes in the evening, which gives you the convenience of becoming a college student while keeping your full-time job.

Low, Low Cost

Forget $20,000. A $2,000 annual tab is too high at most two-year campuses. The average tuition at the nation's two-year colleges in 1997–98 was $1,500. And that's for full-time students. You usually have the option of paying by the course or by the credit hour so that you can work your way into life as a college student slowly and inexpensively.

After you pay the tuition, you'll encounter no other costs, except your books and that gallon of gas a day. No room and board. No fees to support the football team. No shipping and handling.

> The two-year option certainly is worth a glance.

A two-year school education is a full-time education for maybe $1,500 a year. If you are a cost-conscious person, money is a big reason that a two-year college should be on your list.

Don't exclude Bigbucks U. because its annual cost is

Rising Popularity of Community Colleges for Vocational Training

Percentage distribution of sub-baccalaureate students reporting a vocational major according to type of postsecondary instution: 1989–90 and 1995–96

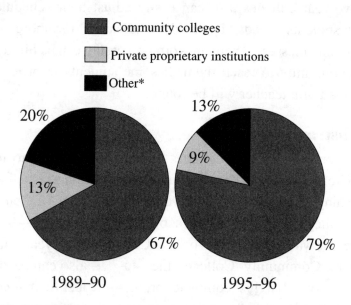

■ Community colleges

▨ Private proprietary institutions

■ Other*

20%   13%   67%   1989–90

13%   9%   79%   1995–96

*Other institution types include public 4-year; private, not-for-profit 4-year; private, not-for-profit less-than-4-year; and public vocational/technical institutions.

NOTE: Percentages may not add to 100 due to rounding.

U.S. Department of Education, National Center for Education Statistics, 1989–90 and 1995–96 National Postsecondary Student Aid Study (NPSAS: 1990 and NPSAS: 1996).

$26,000. You may get $24,500 in financial aid, and the cost to you would be $1,500. But if all else fails, Convenient Community College may be your low-cost backup.

Varied Curriculum

At a typical two-year college, the curriculum is varied and flexible. Course offerings are split roughly 50-50 between the traditional academic stuff (for students going on to four-year schools) and employable skills, such as computer repair, dental hygiene, and travel agentry (for students seeking a job or career change). The full course menu actually can be much larger than at four-year colleges.

Two-year colleges also can easily adjust their schedules to meet students' needs. If the demand arises for more word-processing classes, experts in word processing can be hired from the community to teach them. If some students want to study Latin, a Latin teacher will be found.

Undistracted Faculty

Professors at two-year colleges have only one job—to teach. They're not distracted by more rewarding sidelines, such as researching and writing journal articles, as are many of their four-year-college brethren. When a biology professor walks into a classroom at Convenient Community College, the students know that his complete professional attention that day will be focused on teaching biology.

> Two-year colleges also can easily adjust their schedules to meet students' needs.

Two-year colleges are not stuck in the tradition of four-year colleges that insists a Ph.D. is necessary to teach college courses. Many faculty members at two-year colleges are working experts in their field, holding full-time jobs in addition to teaching a course or two. Anyone who has knowledge—and the ability to share that knowledge—can become a two-year-college teacher.

A Way to Overcome the Bad Times

If you have a high school record that not even your mother can admire, a two-year college is the place to erase it. Just about all public two-year colleges (88 percent of them are public) use open admissions, which means anyone with a high school diploma or its equivalent can enroll. Those Cs and Ds on your transcript won't block your way.

When you earn all As in your two years at a community college, you'll have an impressive record for an admission office on a four-year campus. If Flagship State sees you handling college-level work well, it will forget those bad times you had in high school.

Easy Access to Four-Year Colleges

The paths are well worn. Thousands of students make the trip each year. After earning an associate degree at a two-year college, they move on with little difficulty to work for a bachelor's degree on a four-year campus.

Four-year colleges look to their two-year siblings—especially neighbors in their area—as sources of good students. They're well aware of what students can do if they complete the two-year curriculum. Transferring to a four-year college with a two-year degree can be the easiest way to get there.

In most cases, you still must fill out application forms to get into a four-year college. But even that task is disappearing. In some states, agreements between four-year and two-year schools allow students who pass prescribed courses to move on automatically. This transfer process is just like moving to another campus of the same college. These automatic-admission deals are known in the trade as articulation agreements. If you hear about one at your community college, you're in luck. If you don't, ask.

One Way to Enter a Step at a Time

If you're not sure that you're ready for the rigors of being a full-time college student, you can test the waters gradually, one toe at a time. Take one course at night and see how you do. The next semester, take two. Before you know it, you'll be earning As and be ready to charge into the student business full-time.

Vocational Schools and Apprenticeships

Julianne Dueber

Two education alternatives for teens who decide not to attend college are vocational schools and apprenticeships. Technical and vocational schools provide instruction focusing on a single job or career field. Apprenticeships are programs in which a person becomes an actual employee of a business and receives both pay and on-the-job training. Julianne Dueber lists some advantages and disadvantages of these alternative pathways as well as advice on obtaining more information about specific programs. A former high school teacher, Dueber is the author of *The Ultimate High School Survival Guide*, from which this excerpt was taken.

Four-year college is not the best choice for everyone. Many students attend two-year community colleges or technical schools or obtain on-the-job training through an apprenticeship or internship. No matter which direction you take, you'll need to check out entrance requirements. Keep career interests and your abilities in mind. . . .

Technical and vocational schools that offer vocational training are sometimes called trade schools. They offer a wide variety of training and education that lead to jobs in a single career field. I checked in my local phone book to get an idea of the types of schools out there for you. Here's a few ideas of careers you can be trained for: dental and medical assistant, pet groomer, administrative assistant, medical records technician, computer programmer, computer-aided draftsman, welder, travel agent, office administrator, computer network administrator, health information specialist, bartender, veterinary assistant, furniture reupholsterer, auto mechanic, occupational therapy assistant, massage therapist, and a ton of others. Check your own yellow pages to find other professions that you can obtain training for. . . .

> Four-year college is not the best choice for everyone.

Advantages of Vocational Training

- *Your time in school will most likely range anywhere from one week to two years.* This short term training will allow you to enter the work force quickly.
- *You will train for employment in a specific job.* You should be able to gain employment when you complete the training because your skills will match the job requirements.
- *Your education most likely will not cost you as much as it would to go to a four-year college.*
- *Your teacher will have personal experience in the field he or she is teaching.* He can give you helpful hints for obtaining a job.
- *You will use the knowledge you gain in classes to solve practical problems in laboratories and workshops at your job site.*
- *During your vocational training, you'll get lifelong skills,* such as good work habits, self-confidence, teamwork, and practical problem solving. Training will be hands-on. That is, you'll begin by learning the specific skills necessary for the job.

Possible Disadvantages of Vocational Training

- *You may train for a field for which there are not many jobs available.* You should research careers to see where the jobs are. A helpful resource is the *Occupational Outlook Handbook* of the Bureau of Labor Statistics. The hottest fields will be in the health and home health care, computer programming and systems, occupational and physical therapy, and paralegal fields.

- *Some vocational schools are better than others.* You must check out each school carefully. Talk to past graduates. Find out what percentage of graduates get jobs. Know who you're dealing with. Call the Better Business Bureau to see if there are any complaints against the school. Talk to past graduates. Check to see if they have state licensing and accreditation. Are the courses up-to-date and taught by teachers with the latest skills? Do the facilities have state-of-the-art technology? Does the school have a job placement office? Will you get hands-on training?

- *You won't get as well-rounded an education as you'd get at a traditional college.* You'll be studying only one area. This focus does not have to be a negative, however. You can study additional information on your own by reading books, newspapers, and magazines. Many graduates of vocational schools are avid readers with a lot of knowledge on many topics. Don't buy into stereotypes if you know what field interests you. Go for it! . . .

Apprenticeships

According to the *Occupational Outlook Quarterly*, "Apprenticeship is a relationship between an employer and an employee during which the worker, or apprentice, learns a trade. The apprenticeship covers all aspects of the trade and includes both on-the-job training and related instruction in the classroom. Apprenticeships usually last about 4 years but range from 1 to 6 years. During this time, apprentices work under experienced workers known as journey workers—the status they will attain after successfully completing their apprenticeships."

Apprentices are actual employees of a company, which pays them roughly half of what the experienced worker gets. The apprentices get an increase in pay after satisfactorily completing each portion of the apprentice training.

Typical apprenticeships train you for careers as a carpenter, welder, iron worker, electrician, stone mason, and tile setter, among others. Also, there are a number of different things you can do after you've trained for one of these careers. For example, a carpenter doesn't just hammer nails all day. He's the member of a team that builds homes, commercial buildings, roads, and bridges. He also remodels homes and office buildings, installs drywall and cabinets, and completes exterior and interior finishes. Some carpenters specialize in one phase of the trade, such as installing concrete forms, installing acoustical materials, or driving pile. Millwrights handle, clean, erect, install, and dismantle machinery, equipment, and other heavy materials. Cabinet-makers build specialized, fine cabinets, furniture, and other articles for customers.

> Some vocational schools are better than others. You must check out each school carefully.

Typical Requirements for Apprenticeships

1. You must have a good high school attendance record and a good attitude.
2. You must be drug-free.
3. You must have a good work ethic.
4. You must have reliable transportation and access to a telephone.
5. You should have good math and communication skills.
6. You should like physical work, much of it outdoors.

The U.S. Department of Labor Bureau of Apprenticeships and Training mandates that you spend at least 144 hours per year in the classroom. To be an apprentice, you usually must be 18 years old, unless you get special permission from your parents. Then you may enter an apprentice program at 17. In a number of programs, you don't need a GED or high school diploma.

Advantages of Apprenticeships

- *You won't be stuck behind a desk day after day.* You'll go from job to job, meeting new people and seeing new places.
- *You get paid as soon as you start your apprenticeship.*
- *Many apprenticeship programs are affiliated with community and four-year colleges.* Some community colleges will give you credits for anywhere from 34 to 45 hours toward an associate's degree depending on your experiences. Then, you only need to earn 19 to 30 more credit hours at the community college to get the degree.
- *When you advance to journeyperson, your salary almost doubles.* Wages are based on your level of training and years of experience.

Possible Disadvantages of Apprenticeships

- *You will have some periods where you cannot work, due to the weather.* Sounds like a good time to take a vacation, doesn't it?
- *Your education will be limited to knowledge of one trade.* But this is not always true. Many tradesmen read about things other than their trade. You have the power to educate yourself however you see fit.
- *The tradesman sometimes wishes he had gone to college.* Well, there is nothing stopping him or her from going to night or weekend classes. In fact, apprentices are ideal candidates for distance learning classes via the Internet. . . .

Sources of Information

Talk to the trade unions in your city or town for more information. Your state will most likely have an office that oversees apprenticeships. You may also contact the U.S. Department of Labor's Bureau of Apprenticeship and Training, 200 Constitution Avenue, NW, Washington, D.C. 20212; telephone: 202-219-5943.

Do some research to find more information. Ask your school counselor for helpful phone numbers and sources of information.

Point of Contention: Is Joining the Military a Good Way to Obtain an Education?

Since 1973, when the U.S. government ended the military draft, the U.S. armed services have relied on an all-volunteer force. Recruiters for the branches of the American military (the U.S. Army, Navy, Air Force, Marines, and Coast Guard) have promoted military service as not just a career in itself, but a means to gaining an education. In recent years, the military has been increasing its offers of financial aid and scholarships in order to encourage more young Americans to join.

Students considering the American military have several options. Some attend U.S. Service Academies such as the United States Military Academy in West Point (tuition paid by the government), while others receive scholarships from Reserve Officer Training Corps (ROTC) programs in exchange for six years of military service. The Montgomery GI Bill and the Army and Navy College Fund provide financial aid to students who enlist in one of the military branches or the National Guard.

Two sharply contrasting opinions about whether the military is a good way to obtain an education are presented here. The first is taken from a website operated by the U.S. Department of Defense. The second is by the Central Committee for Conscientious Objectors, an organization that promotes resistance to war and militarism.

Joining the Military Is a Good Way to Obtain an Education

U.S. Department of Defense

Entering the military does not put your life or education on hold. In fact, the opposite can happen. Many who enter the military make rapid educational and career progress. Doors open they never knew existed. And later they realize that their military service was a major factor contributing to their success.

Our technologically sophisticated military needs to attract smart, intelligent recruits. To do this, Today's Military offers a wide variety of programs that help recruits earn college credit, attend college while in the service, and/or provide cash for college tuition. And because these programs are portable, a duty station change won't interrupt your progress towards that degree.

In 1999 alone, over 30,000 college degrees were earned by members of the active duty military through the off-duty, voluntary education program. . . .

Credit Programs

Military School Credits. The military has a network of over 300 schools and over 10,000 courses to train members in the skills necessary for over 4,100 occupations. One well-kept secret is that about 60% of these courses are certified for college credit by the American Council on Education (ACE). That means that you can earn college credits for being trained (at no cost to you) by top military instructors to learn a marketable skill. Note: A credit isn't a credit until it's approved by the college, but if you need help convincing them, ACE makes a help desk available.

Servicemember Opportunity Colleges (SOC). Over

26,000 military members participated in SOC in 1999. It's popular because it's a built-in way to get a college degree—even if your duty station changes. SOC is a group of 1,418 colleges and universities that agree to transfer credits among themselves for military members and their families. Whether you're stationed in Key West, Florida or San Diego, California, you'll be able to continue your college studies via SOC. Coursework is done in the classroom, at a distance by computer, or by mail.

Testing Credits. You don't need to look farther for college credit than the local Base Education Center (most bases have one). There you can take the CLEP examination series (general exams like Mathematics or subject exams like Western Civilization), the DSST subject series, or the well-known Regents examination series. Name the subject and the military probably can test you in it. Pass and you get the credits, usually three credits per subject exam.

Community College of the Air Force (CCAF). Air Force enlisted personnel may earn an associate degree in applied science in job-related fields. These range from Computer Science Technology, Aircraft Armament Systems Technology and Weather Technology to Allied Health Sciences, Paralegal, and Information Management. Every CCAF degree requires courses in your technical job specialty, leadership, management, military studies, general education, and physical education.

Tuition Support Programs

Tuition Assistance. The rising cost of tuition can be hard to manage, but the military's Tuition Assistance Program pays for 75 percent of the cost of tuition or expenses up to a maximum of $187.50 per semester hour credit and a personal maximum of $3,500 per fiscal year per student. Your

25% is a small price to pay for a promising future. This program is the same for active duty members in each military service. Selected military reserve and National Guard units also offer a Tuition Assistance Program, although the benefits may vary from the active duty program.

Montgomery GI Bill. The Montgomery GI Bill offers up to $28,800 in tuition in return for a three-year commitment on active duty. You contribute $100 a month for a year. You get $650 a month for 3 years, 19.5 times what you put in. A very handsome return on investment.

> The Montgomery GI Bill offers up to $28,800 in tuition in return for a three-year commitment on active duty.

You can use the GI Bill for college degree programs but also for certificate programs, flight training, apprenticeship/on-the-job training, and correspondence courses, among others. Members of the military reserves and National Guard are also eligible for the GI Bill, although at reduced rates.

College Fund Programs. Here's another little-known secret with a large payoff. If you enlist in the Army, Navy, Marine Corps, or Coast Guard and become eligible for their College Fund Programs, you'll receive up to $50,000 towards your college tuition when combined with the Montgomery GI Bill upon honorable discharge. If you're awarded the College Fund by the Marine Corps or Coast Guard, you'll receive up to $30,000 combined total. In 1997 alone, over 23,000 young veterans used College Fund programs. Sure, you need to qualify for it, but if you do, there's a pot of gold waiting once you complete your tour of duty.

Loan Repayment Programs. If you've completed college and are weighed down by debt, fear not. In the active duty Army, soldiers can qualify to have their loan repaid by the military at the rate of one-third of the loan for each year of active duty served (maximum loan repayment is $65,000). The Army even helps soldiers pay off student loans they've taken out, provided they attended schools on an approved Perkins, Stafford, or other Department of Education Guaranteed Student Loan.

In the active duty Navy and Air Force, a $10,000 Loan Repayment Program is available. Qualifications include: no prior military service, a high school diploma, and a loan guaranteed under the Higher Education Act of 1965. You must qualify for Navy Nuclear Field or other designated critical rating as defined by the U.S. Navy, and other restrictions apply. If you qualify, though, either of these programs is a great way to get out of debt!

Today's Military, "College Prep," www.todaysmilitary.com. Published by Joint Recruiting Advertising Program of the U.S. Department of Defense.

Joining the Military Is Not a Good Way to Get an Education

Central Committee for Conscientious Objectors

We've all seen the advertisements, "Join the Army and earn up to $40,000 for college." The ads seem to say that if you join the military college is all but paid for. But only 35% of recruits receive any education benefits from the military. Most that do get money receive far less than $40,000.

The Montgomery GI Bill was not created to send you, or anyone else, to school. It was designed to recruit soldiers. It may be all the same to you, as long as you end up with money for college. But why the program was created affects its design and how well it is funded. The Montgomery GI Bill advertises a large amount of money but it has lots of strings attached. The maximum benefit of $40,000 quickly dwindles to $14,375 or $6588 for an alarming number of recruits. Many don't find that out until after they've joined! By then it's much too late. . . .

Read the Fine Print

Advertisements that offer money for college if you join the military are advertising two programs, the Montgomery GI Bill and the Army or Navy College Fund. Almost all enlistees join the Montgomery GI Bill on entering the military. Far fewer enlistees qualify for the higher benefit Army/Navy College Fund and they must also participate in the Montgomery GI Bill.

In order to receive any education benefit there are several conditions that must be met. First, you must contribute $100 per month for the first twelve months of your tour. Those payments must be made for all twelve months and can't be canceled once they're begun. There is no refund of that $1200, ever. Additionally, you must receive an honorable discharge, something that 20% of all veterans don't get.

The maximum benefit you can qualify for under the Montgomery GI Bill is $15,575. To earn a larger benefit, like the $40,000 the military is so fond of advertising, you must qualify for the Army/Navy College Fund. To do this you must score in the top half of the military entry tests and be willing to enter a designated job specialty. These designated Military Occupational Specialties are the most unpopular in the military. The military has a hard time filling them because they have no skills that are transferable to the civilian job market.

> Only 35% of recruits receive any education benefits from the military.

More Obstacles

Even after you've been honorably discharged, you're still a long way from getting that money. Even though you've earned your tuition benefit you probably won't get it all. The military has still more requirements for you to fulfill before you get all of your money. Of course, you must be attending an accredited school. The military's payment plan is based on a four year college schedule: they'll pay you equal portions of your money over 36 months (the equivalent of four academic years of nine months each). This schedule is not flexible! If you, like 56% of veterans using the Montgomery GI Bill, attend a two year school or vocational school you can not receive larger payments over a shorter period of time. That means a two year college graduate will receive only half of the money they have earned!

Even though you earned that money, the Montgomery GI Bill doesn't let you decide how to use it in the way that's best for you. But your argument will fall on deaf ears. The military advertises large amounts of education money but the program is designed so the money is hard to get and harder to use. The inflexibility of the Montgomery GI Bill shows that the military wants to use it to recruit you, not to send you to college.

It Isn't Enough

Even if you qualify for and receive the full $40,000, it isn't worth as much as you might think. While World War II GI Bill participants were able to attend 90% of all schools (public, private, two-year and four-year) with their tuition grant, $40,000 will cover just over one year at some private schools today.

Even state universities cost an average of about $9,000 per year. Your benefits probably won't increase while you're in the military (benefits have been raised twice since the program was begun in 1985). But the cost of education will continue to rise at a rate of 5–10% per year. By the time you finish your tour, your education benefit will be worth a quarter less than when you signed up. It if you don't go to school right after the military, which many people don't, your benefit will become worth less and less.

You need to ask yourself in a serious and realistic way, do you intend to go to college? If yes, you need to have a plan. That plan may include joining the military, but you can see that will work for only a few people. If your plans for going to college seem to be more dream than reality, you need to take a long look at what is really possible. If you're hoping that the military can make an unplanned dream come true, it's not going to happen. Don't forget, you're risking your own money in the Montgomery GI Bill as well. . . .

Education in the Military?
Recruiters also like to talk about educational opportunities while you're in the military. According to recruiters, not only will you learn skill in your job specialty but you also have the chance to take college courses on-base or close by. In theory, this may be true. But when the military commissioned a study to see what soldiers thought of military recruiting, an overwhelming number responded that they thought military advertisements' promises of education were "lies . . . false" or "not the truth to me." Rather than working with the helicopters you see in slick advertisements, they found themselves "buffin' floors and pickin' up cigarette butts."

Your decision about whether to join the military, with or without the Montgomery GI Bill, is not an easy one. Unfortunately, it's not as simple as weighing the pros and cons of this or that benefit. Other jobs may be hard to come by, but they don't demand what the military demands. You give up your freedom when you join the military, entering a different world with different laws, where others can control your life 24 hours a day, seven days a week.

The Military Mission

Above all else, the military is an institution with one overriding purpose: to prepare for and fight wars. You literally sign your life over to the military. For some who joined the military before the Gulf War, they didn't fully realize this until they were faced with an actual war in Saudi Arabia against Iraq. Don't make the same mistake they made. If you're going to join the military be prepared to fight a war, even a war you may not agree with. It could be a war we lose, like Vietnam. Or, it could be a war we win, like in Kuwait. Either way, people are killed and you might be the one who kills them. As much as the war in Iraq has been celebrated, you can find US veterans who can't forget some of the awful things they saw there. Is that the kind of risk you want to take to finance your college education?

Be a Smart Consumer

Nobody else can make decisions about what is best for you, not the recruiter and not us. But your decisions should be based on more than slick ads and a recruiter's sales pitch. The military promises but often it does not deliver.

Organizations and Websites

The editors have compiled the following list of organizations concerned with the issues debated in this book. The descriptions are derived from materials provided by the organizations. All have publications or information available for interested readers. The list was compiled on the date of publication of the present volume; the information provided here may change. Be aware that many organizations take several weeks or longer to respond to inquiries, so allow as much time as possible.

The CollegeBound Network

1200 South Ave. #202, Staten Island, NY 10314
(718) 761-4800 • fax: (718) 761-4800
e-mail: information@collegebound.net
website: www.collegebound.net

Founded in 1987, the company provides a variety of online and print resources for high school students seeking information on getting into and succeeding at college. These include *College Bound* magazine and a network of websites aimed at college-bound teens.

CollegeLink.com

55 Green St., Clinton, MA 01510
(800) 394-0404
e-mail: col-user@collegelink.com • website: www.collegelink.com

CollegeLink.com is a computerized college application service in which students can create and send applications online to multiple schools using one online form. Its website features numerous articles and information pieces on selecting colleges, many of which are written by students.

Peterson's
Princeton Pike Corporate Center
2000 Lenox Dr., Lawrenceville, NJ 08648
(609) 896-1800

Peterson's, a division of the Thomson Corporation, provides books and web-based products that provide information about colleges, tests, financial aid, and other matters relating to education.

U.S. Department of Education
400 Maryland Ave. SW, Washington, DC 20202-0498
(800) 872-5327
website: www.ed.gov

The Department's mission is to ensure equal access to education and to promote educational excellence for all American students. Its publications include *Early Childhood Digest, Education Statistics Quarterly*, and hundreds of reports, pamphlets, and other publications. Its website features advice and information directed at students as well as teachers and parents on primary, secondary, college, and vocational education.

Websites

Campusaccess.com
www.campusaccess.com

Campusaccess.com, devised and designed by students, provides information on topics of concern to Canadian high school and college students.

Myfuture.com

www.myfuture.com

The website, a public service of the Department of Defense, provides information on opportunities in the American military branches as well as general information on education and careers.

NextStepMagazine.com

www.nextstepmagazine.com

This companion site to *Next Step Magazine* features numerous articles about college and other topics for high school students.

Teen Ink

http://teenink.com

Teen Ink is an online magazine featuring articles by teen authors; its website includes articles and information about education and college.

Teen Learning Network

www.teenlearningnetwork.com

The website provides a wealth of information both on college and college alternatives.

WhereYouHeaded.com

www.whereyouheaded.com

The website provides information to students and their families on selecting colleges and on taking time off between high school and college; additional services and counseling are available for a fee.

Bibliography

Books

Julianne Dueber — *The Ultimate High School Survival Guide.* Princeton, NJ: Peterson's, 1999.

William J. Ekeler, ed. — *The Black Student's Guide to High School Success.* Westport, CT: Greenwood, 1997.

Bryna J. Fireside — *Choices for the High School Graduate: A Survival Guide for the Information Age.* Chicago, IL: Ferguson, 1999.

Greg Gottesman and Daniel Baer — *College Survival: A Crash Course for Students by Students.* New York: Macmillan, 1999.

Colin Hall and Ron Lieber — *Taking Time Off.* New York: The Noonday Press, 1996.

Linda Lee — *Success Without College.* New York: Broadway Books, 2001.

Joyce Slayton Mitchell — *Winning the Heart of College Admissions Dean: An Expert's Advice for Getting Into College.* Berkeley: Ten Speed Press, 2001.

Pat Ordovensky — *College Planning for Dummies.* Foster City, CA: IDG Books, 1999.

Loren Pope

Looking Beyond the Ivy League: Finding the College That's Right for You. New York: Penguin USA, 1996.

Mike Riera

Surviving High School: Making the Most of the High School Years. Berkeley: Celestial Arts, 1997.

Gail Stewart

The Other America: Teen Dropouts. San Diego: Lucent Books, 1998.

Elizabeth Vollstadt

Teen Issues: Teen Dropouts. San Diego: Lucent Books, 1999.

Ruth K. Westheimer and Pierre Lehu

Dr. Ruth's Guide to College Life. Lanham: MD: Madison Books, 2000.

Periodicals

Karen W. Arenson

"Early Decisions," *New York Times Upfront*, February 11, 2002.

David Boesel

"College for All?" *Education Digest*, November 1999.

James Bowman

"The Graduates," *National Review*, May 17, 1999.

Business Week

"Second Thoughts on Early Decision," March 11, 2002.

Jessica Fladvid

"An Early Grad Suffers Withdrawl," *New York Times Upfront*, March 19, 2001.

Caitlin Flanagan

"Confessions of a Prep School College Counselor," *Atlantic Monthly*, September 2001.

Barbara Kantrowitz   "The New College Game: Roll the Dice, Pick Up a Card. Will Ditch-Digging in Peru or Perfect SATs Let You Skip a Turn and Go Straight to Harvard?" *Newsweek*, April 8, 2002.

Tami Luhby   "Is College Worth It?" *Careers & Colleges*, November 2000.

Brigid McMenamin   "Who Needs College!" *Forbes*, December 28, 1998.

Newsweek   "Curing Senioritis," December 11, 2000.

Ginger Packert   "Apprenticeships for the 21st Century," *Phi Delta Kappan*, June 1996.

Elizabeth Shaw   "Is This What Life's About? I'm Pushing Myself So Hard to Get into a 'Good' College There's No Time to Sleep or Have Fun," *Newsweek*, May 5, 1997.

Alicia M. Sitley   "How to Use College Admission Trends," *Career World*, February 2001.

Greg Smith   "Dealing with Rejection," *Career World*, November/December 2001.

Jonathan Whitbourne   "The Dropout Dilemma: One in Four College Freshmen Drop Out. What Is Going on Here? What Does It Take to Stay In?" *Careers & Colleges*, March 2002.

Index